Serving the New Majority Student

Serving the New Majority Student

Working from Within to Transform the Institution

Edited by Eric Malm and Marguerite Weber

ROWMAN & LITTLEFIELD
Lanham • Boulder • New York • London

Published by Rowman & Littlefield
An imprint of The Rowman & Littlefield Publishing Group, Inc.
4501 Forbes Boulevard, Suite 200, Lanham, Maryland 20706
https://rowman.com

Unit A, Whitacre Mews, 26-34 Stannary Street, London SE11 4AB,
United Kingdom

British Library Cataloguing in Publication Information Available

Library of Congress Cataloging-in-Publication Data Available

ISBN 978-1-4758-3600-4 (hardcover : alk. paper)
ISBN 978-1-4758-3601-1 (pbk. : alk. paper)
ISBN 978-1-4758-3602-8 (electronic)

∞ ™ The paper used in this publication meets the minimum requirements of American
National Standard for Information Sciences Permanence of Paper for Printed Library
Materials, ANSI/NISO Z39.48-1992.

Printed in the United States of America

Contents

Preface

Much of higher education was originally designed to meet the needs of full-time eighteen- to twenty-two-year-old students who enter directly from high school. However, the new majority of our students are older, are likely to swirl among institutions, and have significant adult responsibilities outside of the classroom. The two companion books *Academic Transformation: A Design Approach for the New Majority* and *Serving the New Majority Student: Working from Within to Transform the Institution* are a call to transform colleges and universities to meet the academic and student-experience needs of New Majority students and for adult educators to become advocates, allies, and resources for needed reforms.

Book contributors, including faculty, staff, and administrators at public, private, and community colleges, provide insights for this transformation. Taking a personalized approach based on a wide range of experiences, the contributors provide a framework for cross-campus conversations and collaborations to help stakeholders across the institution to understand New Majority learners' strengths, needs, and challenges within an increasingly competitive educational market.

Academic Transformation: A Design Approach for the New Majority begins with a description of New Majority learners, explores enrollment management and student-experience considerations, articulates a retention model and adapted high-impact practices to support student success, navigates technology considerations, and addresses the impact of academic transformation for New Majority learners on higher education finance.

Serving the New Majority Student: Working from Within to Transform the Institution uses a business perspective to academic transformation, providing a guide for how universities can redefine and restructure their educational product to meet student needs. Taking a human-centered approach, the contributors provide frameworks and examples of how institutions can reallocate technology, effort (internal, external, student, and faculty), and finances to reimagine programs and ensure long-term institutional health.

ONE

Serving the New Majority Student

Eric Malm

A NEW WORLD OF HIGHER EDUCATION

We are entering a new world. Stories about new educational models, which represent both opportunity and threat to educational institutions, are everywhere. A recent Inside Higher Education collection called *Evolving Economic Models for Higher Ed* gives a glimpse at many of the issues.[1] Declining numbers of college-bound high school seniors, increased competition from alternative education providers, decreased funding, and rising costs are among many pressures that institutions face. What educational technology (EdTech) investors view as perhaps one of the most profitable digital investment sectors, many in traditional institutions see as a huge threat.[2] However the future unfolds, it is clear that higher education is entering a new world.

When an institution is under attack, it is natural to identify external threats and consider how those threats may impact existing structures and practices. Of course, people's jobs and livelihoods are at risk. The rise of for-profit universities that run almost entirely on adjunct faculty can frighten tenured faculty at traditional universities. The growth of online programming threatens to increase the reliance on "flexible" contingent faculty.[3] Faculty fear about the long-term sustainability of the tenure system is warranted, as are concerns about the quality and relevance of a college degree.

The uncertainty about the future of higher education isn't limited to those inside universities. A recent Gallup poll found that 56 percent of Democrats and only 33 percent of Republicans were "quite confident" or had a "great deal of confidence" in higher education.[4] Some attribute the

1

declining confidence in a college degree with cost, the employment benefits of a degree, or suspicion about what is being taught and by whom.
Whatever the cause, a perceived irrelevance of higher education by the
public-at-large would be a dangerous thing.

WORKING FROM WITHIN

In this defensive atmosphere, it would be easy to become discouraged,
feel that the future of education is bleak, or lose hope. However, the
future is not bleak. Education is becoming more widely available than
ever, both in the United States and abroad, and will continue to grow.
Questions like "Who will teach?," "Who will learn?," "How will learning
be paid for?," and "What modalities will be used?" become ever more
important. We are not entering another Dark Age, but education *is* evolving. The contributors to this book believe that faculty, staff, and administrators can work together to make the changes needed to remain relevant
in an evolving marketplace.

This book is intended to help facilitate discussions on campus about
institutional transformation. From a business perspective, the need to
adapt is clear. Faced with disruptive new and potential entrants, universities feel pressured to respond. Changing student characteristics and
needs further challenge universities to rethink when, where, and how
instruction takes place. And cost competition from alternative providers
has forced deep consideration of the sustainability of "business as usual."

Together we can work from within to identify opportunities for
change and improvement. But working from within also requires us to
more closely examine the students we have today and the characteristics
and lives of students that we are likely to have in the future. This book
focuses on the attributes and needs of the new majority of students across
the nation. Learning to serve these students will be central to the success
of many institutions.

WHO IS THE NEW MAJORITY?

Within the university and the admissions office, *traditional* students are
those who are eighteen, start college immediately after high school graduation, and are first-time, full-time students typically enrolled in fifteen
to eighteen credit-hours per semester. More often than not, they are residential students, are engaged in campus activities, and probably have a
part-time job on or off campus. These students will want to remain on
track to graduate in four years, at which point they will eagerly move on
to their careers.

Many faculty, when thinking of students, think of first-time, full-tim-
ers, who are mainly interested in being good students and having fun

while they are in school. For those of us who are teachers, we expect *our* class to be their top priority. If these students stick to their knitting, we expect them to graduate in four years (or three and a half, if they're really motivated) and then move out into the adult world after graduation. We assume that the majority of our students fit into this category.

The second admissions term of interest to us is the *nontraditional student*, but even these are somewhat traditional, too, in that we use this term to describe adults returning as students, students who are older than twenty-four, perhaps veterans, part-time students, and commuters. Some institutions have special academic units for adult learners, continuing-education offices and night and weekend classes to "accommodate" them as students. We also know that there are nontraditional students in our classrooms, but at most institutions, the attention is squarely on the traditional undergraduate student. We have designed our entire institution—from recruiting and enrollment, to residence life, financial aid, academic support, and career services—around the eighteen- to twenty-two-year-old student who has come to us directly from high school.

We need to move beyond the terms *traditional* and *nontraditional* because campus demographics along with students' expectations for the value and benefits of higher education have changed. As costs have increased, so have the financial pressures that students face. Today about 40 percent of full-time undergraduates twenty-four or younger worked, and more than 75 percent of part-time students age twenty-four or younger worked.[5] A recent study suggests that 82 percent of undergraduates couldn't afford to go to school without working.[6] And time spent working isn't the only challenge students face, as we'll see later in the chapter.

In this book we define a new category, the New Majority (illustrated in figure 1.1), to help focus attention on the fact that our student population has changed in significant ways. We posit the New Majority as consisting of two different groups: working adults ages twenty-five or older pursuing an undergraduate degree, and students ages eighteen to twenty-four who are going to school *and* have significant adult responsibilities. Although there are many ways of viewing and quantifying adult responsibilities, in figure 1.1 we break them down into financial independence and "other" adult responsibilities (such as having dependents).

The New Majority now represents more than half of total undergraduate students and will continue to grow in number. But this significant change has not yet been fully realized or absorbed by stakeholders in higher education. The purpose of this book is to better describe the New Majority, illustrate how these students are driving change in the education marketplace, and provide a context for institution-wide conversations about change.

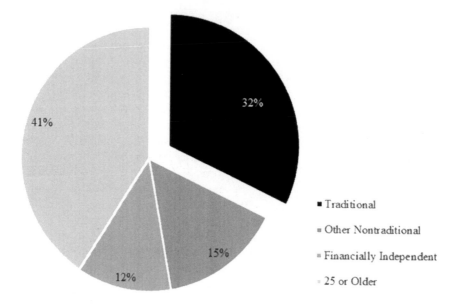

Figure 1.1. The New Majority
Source: **Author's calculations using data from National Center for Education Statistics, PowerStat Data Retrieval Tool (2016), https://nces.ed.gov/datalab/powerstats/default.aspx; National Center for Education Statistics,** *Digest of Education Statistics,* **2014 Tables (2014), https://nces.ed.gov/programs/digest/d14/tables/dt14_303.40.asp; and US Department of Education,** *Demographic and Enrollment Characteristics of Nontraditional Undergraduates: 2011–2012* **(2015), https://nces.ed.gov/pubs2015/2015025.pdf.**

REALLY? . . . IN MY CLASS?

It's a surprise to many that the New Majority is, in fact, the majority of undergraduates today. Let's first examine the expanding pool of adult learners. According to the National Center for Education Statistics, in 2013 there were about 8.1 million undergraduate students ages twenty-five or older, representing more than 40 percent of the approximately 20 million undergraduate students enrolled that year.[7]

But what exactly do we mean by *traditionally aged students with adult responsibilities*, and how do these responsibilities differ from those of the past? The growing importance and impact of these adult responsibilities has been studied for several years. Table 1.1, adapted from a widely cited Department of Education study, shows the percentage of students who fell into each of six categories that marked a student as *nontraditional.*[8] As you'll see, although the percentages vary significantly by institution type, they are significant (and perhaps surprising). This data start to paint a picture of a student population that may be "hiding" among our traditionally aged students and are students who have significant financial and family responsibilities.

So how many "traditional" students do we have left? Although the numbers depend on how attributes like financial independence are defined, a report from the American Council on Education (ACE) suggests that as few as 15 percent of undergraduates still fit in the traditional label.[9] Other research finds that about half of students are independent, about 25 percent are parents, about 15 percent are single parents, more than a quarter are employed full-time, and nearly 40 percent are employed part-time.[10] Between 2005 and 2015, the cost of tuition and room and board increased by 33 percent at public institutions and 26 percent at private institutions, after adjusting for inflation.[11] With today's high tuition costs, fewer and fewer students can afford the luxury of attending college full-time without working.

Anecdotally, professors will tell you students are changing. When students don't seem to be as focused or engaged as we would hope, what's a teacher to do? We could complain about students' not being responsible, about the admissions department, or about an ineffective K–12 system. Or we could learn to change to better serve these student–customers. Whether one takes the business view that students are our customers and we need to produce a product that works for them, or whether we view it as the job of higher education to produce well-informed citizens who possess critical-thinking and information-literacy skills necessary to contribute to society, it's becoming clear that institutions need to find more effective ways of serving our students.

Table 1.1 Undergraduates with Nontraditional Characteristics by Type of Institution (%)

Type of Institution	Financially Independent	Attended Part Time	Delayed Enrollment	Worked Full Time	Had Dependents	Single Parent
Total	**50.9**	**47.9**	**45.5**	**39.3**	**26.9**	**13.3**
Public 2-year	63.7	69.5	58.7	53.8	34.5	16.4
Public 4-year	37.6	33.3	31.5	25.5	17.6	9.2
Private nonprofit 4-year	36.7	27.6	34.0	28.5	18.8	8.6
Private for-profit	72.9	21.5	67.8	40.8	44.3	26.6
Total	50.9	47.9	45.5	39.3	26.9	13.3

Source: Adapted from S. Choy, *Nontraditional Undergraduates*, National Center for Educational Statistics, table 2, http://nces.ed.gov/pubs2002/2002012.pdf.

EVIDENCE OF A PROBLEM

Although there are clearly many factors that contribute to low completion rates, the factors that today's adult and independent students face
make completion increasingly difficult. Studies of noncompletion show
financial and employment issues as being the main reasons students
stopped their education before completing their degree.[12] There is a clear
similarity in the reasons for noncompletion cited in figure 1.2 and the
attributes of the nontraditional student. Family and financial issues can
be difficult to balance in our traditional setting.

Low degree-completion rates are one sign that many students are not
being adequately served. Nationally, 58 percent of students who enter a
full-time four-year program graduate within six years. Students entering
less selective colleges with open enrollment complete degrees just 34 percent of the time within six years, and 27 percent at for-profit institutions.[13] Although there are certainly many factors that impact degree
completion, when students start college but walk away without a degree,
institutions should be concerned. And lack of completion today means an
increasing population of adults who are likely to return in the future,
perhaps discouraged and in debt. With around 31 million students who
started college in the past twenty years but did not earn a degree,[14] it's
clear that the ranks of the New Majority will continue to increase.

Student debt burdens are another sign of a problem. In 2016, the average debt of graduating students was $25,902 for public four-year institu-

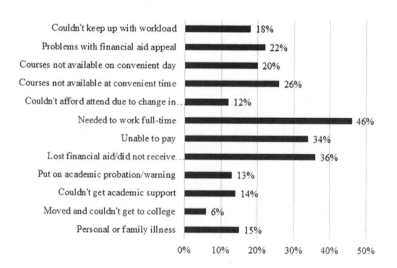

Figure 1.2. Reasons for Noncompletion, Ivy Tech Community College, 2013
Source: **Sonia Ninon,** *Non-Returning Students Survey Results.* **Indianapolis, IN:
Ivy Technical College, 2013.**

tions and $29,657 for private four-year institutions with 60 percent and 64 percent of students, respectively, graduating with debt. And debt without a degree is even a tougher problem. An analysis by Education Policy found that in 2009, 54 percent of students in for-profit institutions dropped out, which is an increase of 20 percentage points from 2001.[15] So although many adult students are choosing for-profit institutions and community colleges, completion rates are low and the percentage of students leaving college with debt but no degree is too high.

The pressures faced by the learners with adult responsibilities, such as work and family commitments, also reveal themselves in the enrollment choices students are making. Figure 1.3 shows undergraduate enrollment by student age and institution type. Although the for-profit sector is still small in absolute numbers, a large percentage of their student–customers are adult learners. We see that the more agile for-profit institutions are disproportionately attracting older students, many of whom prefer more flexibly structured classes.

As students have searched for convenience and affordability, enrollment in online courses has increased. Figure 1.4 shows the number of students taking at least one online course from 2002 to 2012, growing from 9.6 percent to 33.5 percent of students. The growth and change in the course formats that students choose to take also reinforce the idea that these students face a variety of competing needs, and more flexibly formatted online and hybrid courses may meet their needs. These choices

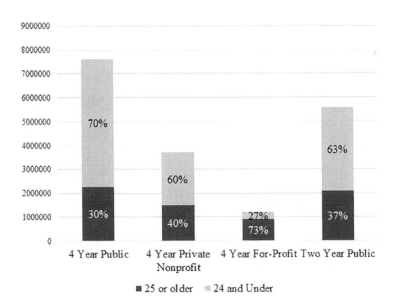

Figure 1.3. Undergraduate Enrollment by Student Age and Institution Type
Source: **National Student Clearinghouse Research Center, 2016.**

may be driven more by cost and convenience and may not actually provide the highest levels of learning. Administrators are concerned with low course-completion rates for online courses, so the migration to online programs should be viewed with caution.[16]

HOW ARE NEW MAJORITY LEARNERS DIFFERENT?

It's not just the lifestyles and challenges that make New Majority learners different. Mind-set is also important. Although some traditional undergraduates may consider themselves "students who work," New Majority students may view themselves as "employees who study."[17] This distinction illustrates student mind-set. Do students view themselves first as students or as workers? The distinction has impacts in the classroom. Students who view themselves as workers first, may lack confidence in themselves as students. Professors who can leverage the knowledge and experience from the work world are likely to help these employees who study to achieve more. But this requires both a realization on the part of faculty and a shift in teaching and assignment styles.

Adults who have started but not completed college have been the focus of numerous foundation and government studies. Researchers understand important ways in which adult learners are different and many of the types of practices that can more effectively help these students succeed. A report by Erisman and Steel (2015) on Lumina Founda-

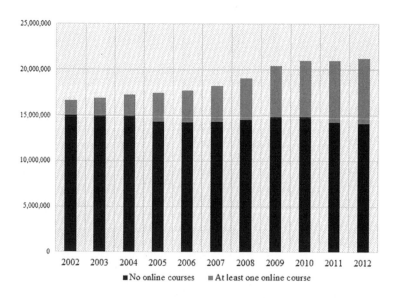

Figure 1.4. Students Taking at Least One Online Course
Source: **National Student Clearinghouse Research Center, 2016.**

tion adult-completion efforts asserts that "the problem is that this knowledge about the differences between traditional college students and adult learners has not been factored into the pedagogy and operations of nearly enough colleges and universities . . . , [and] adults returning to college to complete a degree need a higher education system that is more affordable, flexible and student-centered than the one that currently exists."[18]

Erisman and Steel's (2015) analysis points to several broad categories of need. Adult students need particular kinds of outreach and recruitment efforts. Adults who are near completion are surprisingly difficult to reach to make the case to return to studies, but strides have been made to communicate with these students more effectively. Once in the pipeline, student support services are critical. Issues like determining credit transfer and credit for prior learning are important, as are conversations about financial and academic support. Academic programs need to be structured with a focus on how degree completion can be linked to career success. At the course level, flexibility is important, as is the ability to leverage student strengths to boost confidence and accelerate completion. Technology plays an important role in making the whole experience more accessible and dynamic.

WORKING FROM WITHIN TO TRANSFORM THE INSTITUTION

The chapters in this book put the practitioner-focused ideas about teaching, technology, administration, and support services (that were discussed in depth in the book *Academic Transformation: A Design Approach for the New Majority*) into a business context. The *Academic Transformation* book focuses on specific actions that can be taken by departments across campus to work together to better serve New Majority learners. This book goes further, and challenges institutional stakeholders to think about these issues from a business perspective. Although some readers may resist descriptions of education as a business, we feel this is an important and needed discussion.

Rather than viewing the changing landscape of education as an ominous or negative thing, we believe that by focusing on today's New Majority learner, we can improve levels of learning while remaining competitive in a changing environment. The value of this book will be in the conversations that take place once people are aware of the important ways in which the New Majority is already transforming higher education. Working and talking together, we believe that institutions can be transformed from within.

KEY POINTS

- The world of higher education is changing as it faces the impact of new technologies and more diverse students' needs.
- Full-time students ages eighteen to twenty-two represent less than half of undergraduate students nationally, yet colleges and universities are still designed primarily around these students.
- New Majority students tend to be older but also include traditionally aged students with significant adult responsibilities. Because New Majority students aren't always older, they may be "hidden" among a traditionally aged population.
- The contributors of this book believe that stakeholders can work together from within higher education to adapt to changing markets and increasingly diverse needs of the New Majority population.

NOTES

1. Inside Higher Education and Wiley Educational Services, "Evolving Economic Models for Higher Ed," https://edservices.wiley.com/ihe-booklet-econ-models.

2. R. Shulman, "Global EdTech Investments and Outlook: 10 EdTech Companies You Should Know About," *Forbes*, May 17, 2017, https://www.forbes.com/sites/robynshulman/2017/05/17/global-edtech-investments-and-outlook-10-edtech-companies-you-should-know-about/#b07c4cb5bb30.

3. AAUP, "Contingent Faculty Positions," https://www.aaup.org/issues/contingency.

4. Gallup, "Why Are Republicans Down on Higher Ed?" Poll, August 16, 2017, http://www.gallup.com/poll/216278/why-republicans-down-higher.aspx.

5. National Center for Education Statistics, "College Student Employment," http://nces.ed.gov/programs/coe/indicator_ssa.asp.

6. P. Attewell and D. Lavin, "The Other 75%: College Education beyond the Elite," in *What Is College For? The Public Purpose of Higher Education*, ed. E. C. Langemann and H. Lewis (New York: Teachers College Press, 2012), 86–102.

7. National Center for Educational Statistics, "Characteristics of Postsecondary Students," https://nces.ed.gov/programs/coe/indicator_csb.asp.

8. S. Choy, *Nontraditional Undergraduates*, National Center for Educational Statistics, http://nces.ed.gov/pubs2002/2002012.pdf.

9. L. Soares, *Post-traditional Learners and the Transformation of Postsecondary Education: A Manifesto for College Leaders*, American Council on Education, http://www.acenet.edu/news-room/Documents/Post-traditional-Learners.pdf.

10. http://www.clasp.org/resources-and-publications/publication-1/CPES-Nontraditional-students-pdf.pdf.

11. https://nces.ed.gov/fastfacts/display.asp?id=76.

12. S. Ninon, *Non-Returning Students Survey Results* (Indianapolis, IN: Ivy Technical College, 2013).

13. https://nces.ed.gov/fastfacts/display.asp?id=40.

14. National Student Clearinghouse Research Center, *Some College, No Degree: A National View of Students with Some College Enrollment, But No Completion*, https://nscresearchcenter.org/signaturereport7.

15. Education Policy Center, "Degreeless in Debt: What Happens to Borrowers Who Drop Out," http://educationpolicy.air.org/publications/degreeless-debt-what-happens-borrowers-who-drop-out.

16. Soares, *Post-traditional Learners and the Transformation of Postsecondary Education.*

17. Soares, *Post-traditional Learners and the Transformation of Postsecondary Education.*

18. W. Erisman and P. Steele, *Adult College Completion in the 21st Century: What We Know and What We Don't,* Higher Education Insight, 2015.

TWO

Higher Educational Offerings, Business Models, and the New Majority

Beth Rubin

Universities are complex organizations that provide a number of different products and services for their stakeholders, and institutions have developed a common structure that allows them to provide those outcomes. However, because of the changing nature of the student body, new technologies, and changes in state and federal funding, there is a growing range of higher-educational offerings and resulting university business models and structures.

First and foremost, universities provide knowledge and skills to undergraduate students that they need to be successful adults, employees, and citizens. The Lumina Foundation has identified five categories of proficiencies that are developed by postsecondary education: (1) broad integrative knowledge of social sciences, humanities, and sciences; (2) specialized knowledge of the specific field in which they major; (3) intellectual skills that can be applied in any situation, including analytical inquiry, quantitative fluency, ethical reasoning, and communicative fluency; (4) applied and collaborative learning; and (5) civic and global learning.[1] These categories hold for the associate, bachelor, and master levels, at increasing levels of complexity.[2]

A second major service provided by universities is the development of new knowledge through research. This takes a great deal of the time of most faculty in large universities, supported by the work of doctoral students, who contribute to research and usually receive stipends that provide financial support for their graduate education. Although some faculty obtain grants from the federal government or private agencies to support their research and pay these stipends, a large portion of research costs is funded by universities. The result is that many of the costs of supporting research are provided by undergraduate tuition.[3]

Another output of universities is their support and provision of services for organizations and people in the communities around them. This includes everything from counseling services to expertise and resources to aid the development of small businesses. According to one estimate, the University of Minnesota contributed $390 million to the state over five years through patents, licensing, royalties, and business spin-offs, in addition to $204 million annually in direct service and charitable work.[4]

Traditional universities also provide services, including a relatively safe and supervised place for young adults to grow up. In the idealized situation, parents pay tuition for four years to send their children to a center of higher learning, where they develop responsibility as well as intellectual skills, and where they step gradually from life in a dormitory to living on their own. A corollary benefit is the development of social capital through networks of alumni who provide opportunities such as internships, jobs, and funding for students. However, as the costs of university have risen and the nature of the student body has changed, this phenomenon of parentally supported development into debt-free adulthood is increasingly rare.

CHANGES IN TECHNOLOGY, FUNDING, AND COSTS

The environment in which universities operate is going through massive change. The nature of the student body is almost completely different, as described in the introduction to this volume. Several other environmental changes also affect universities, including the availability of new technology, cuts in state and federal funding, and increases in costs involved in traditional academic activities.

Information technology has gone through a revolution in the last twenty years. The Internet has changed from a system used by researchers and the intellectual elite to a system used by the majority of Americans. Computing power continues to double every two years, and ever-faster and more sophisticated computers complete with built-in video cameras, speakers, and microphones are available for a few hundred dollars. As of summer 2016, more than 88 percent of Americans use the Internet from home.[5]

These innovations enable multichannel communication through computers around the country and the world. Approximately 400 million people play massive multiplayer online games (MMOG) over the Internet, such as World of Warcraft, interacting with both friends and strangers in a shared experience.[6] More than 1.6 billion people share ideas, events, images, and videos through social-media tools such as Facebook.[7]

The same technological infrastructure allows students to learn together, and faculty to teach, in highly interactive classes over the Internet. Students collaborate in classes, groups, and dyads; hold both asynchronous and synchronous discussions and chats; develop joint reports and projects; share ideas; and critique one another. Faculty design courses, guide discussions, lead classes, and provide detailed formative feedback through video recordings, audio recordings, and text feedback.

Other aspects of the environment have also changed. The costs of providing higher education have increased significantly, while state funding has declined.[8] The cost of maintaining a library has increased; for example, the cost of reference books rose from an average of $40.92 in 1989 to an average of $72.31 in 2015.[9] The cost of journals has risen much more, increasing 41 percent in only five years, from 2010 to 2015.[10] The cost of an average journal has increased 188 percent from 1986 to 2004. As the number of academic journals has also increased, overall spending of research-supporting libraries on academic journals increased a whopping 273 percent from 1986.[11]

An analysis by the University of Illinois Libraries found that administrative expenses in universities have also increased because schools are required to hire more staff to comply with rules and guidelines such as diversity support staff. In addition, university presidents report that traditionally aged students expect high-end luxuries such as sushi bars and climbing walls, whereas faculty expect smaller teaching loads and more support for research, adding to costs.[12]

Although the costs of operating universities have increased, most states have sharply reduced their funding of higher education; from 2009 to 2014, per-student spending declined in all states but two, continuing a trend that began in the 1980s.[13] After adjusting for inflation, state spending per student has decreased on average 20.3 percent, or $1,805, from 2008 to 2015.[14] In the longer term, the decrease has been even greater, with an inflation-adjusted decrease of 28 percent in state support per student, from the year 2000 through 2014.[15]

As a result of greater expenses and lower funding levels, the cost of tuition has increased nearly 30 percent since the recession of 2008.[16] At four-year public universities, tuition costs have increased an average of 33 percent, or $2,333, with some states increasing tuition by more than 60 percent.[17] In addition, federal funding for research has declined by 15.4 percent from 2010 to 2014, a decline of $20 billion; almost one-third of that is directed to university research (nearly $6 billion).[18] Although federal funding such as Pell grants have increased, they have not increased enough to offset the higher costs. This creates a growing barrier for adult students who must pay for their college.

THE EXPANSION OF HIGHER-EDUCATION LEARNING PRODUCTS

As a result of the massive changes in students, funding, costs, and technology over the last twenty years, there have been many innovations in the types of postsecondary offerings available to the public. Students who are older, have families, and work don't need a place to grow up as "traditional" unencumbered eighteen- to twenty-one-year-olds do. They have less need for the fitness centers, climbing walls, sushi bars, and fountains. This, along with the growing costs of traditional university structures and the many new affordances of technology, allow entrepreneurial organizations to provide new kinds of higher-educational services, such as online learning, massive online open courses (MOOCs), boot camps, and competence-based learning.

Online Learning Options

The vast majority of postsecondary institutions now offer online learning options,[19] and online course enrollments continue to increase year by year.[20] These courses allow students flexibility in their location and in the timing of classes because most are asynchronous; students have deadlines but do not have to adhere to a specific class time and day. This combination allows traditionally aged students to take courses from home in the summer and those who work to take courses throughout the year.

If institutional policies allow it, online courses allow for greater scale because full-time faculty can develop course materials, and part-time faculty or graduate students can teach them. This can create greater standardization across sections, opportunities for instructors to collaborate on course materials, and higher levels of course quality. Instructional designers often support course development, and the use of imagery, video, and student-centered pedagogy can lead to greatly improved course design and enhanced student experiences.[21]

The skills needed to market online programs to a geographically distributed audience are new to most university departments of enrollment management, just as the skills needed to develop and teach online courses are not held by most professors. To support the growth in online learning, an entire industry of organizations that support the development of online learning has developed.

Many nonprofit and public universities work with vendors such as Pearson/Embanet, Wiley/Deltak, Keypath, and similar organizations to help them market online programs, develop online courses, and support students.[22] For-profit universities such as the University of Phoenix, Capella, and Kaplan, on the other hand, generally develop these skills in house and dedicate large sums of money to advertising and marketing their programs.

Competency-Based Education

Another approach to providing flexibility in higher education is the move to competency-based education (CBE). CBE refers to universities awarding academic credit for demonstration of "competence," or the mastery of specific skills, knowledge, and abilities, rather than awarding credit based on the amount of time spent in class. There are different approaches to CBE; some require students to complete formal courses, and others do not. But all involve identifying specific competencies that students must master to earn academic credit and directly assessing those competencies.[23]

Some universities are based largely, if not completely, around CBE; for example, Western Governors University is a private nonprofit university established in 1998,[24] in which all credit is awarded based on assessments of competence. Students pay a flat fee for a specific time frame (six months) and can obtain as many credits during that time as they can demonstrate mastery of. They can test out of segments or entire courses where they have already mastered the requisite skills, or they may take courses and study learning resources to develop them.

Other universities have followed similar paths, including Excelsior College, Southern New Hampshire University, Northern Arizona, and the University of Wisconsin's Flexible Options program. Many other universities offer CBE for some programs, and some require that students take full courses that last a specific time frame but measure competence directly to determine college credit.[25]

In recent years, CBE has become accepted by a growing number of higher-educational institutions.[26] The expansion of CBE was supported by an independent research and advocacy organization called the Lumina Foundation, which developed a set of standardized competences that reflect general abilities developed through different levels of higher education. The "Degree Qualifications Profile" includes descriptions of five categories of general academic competencies at the associate, bachelor, and master levels.[27] Some of these competencies, such as reading, writing, and critical thinking, can be assessed by newly developed standardized tests such as the Educational Testing Service's Proficiency Profile.[28]

Prior Learning Assessment

Universities that cater to adult students recognize that many already have well-developed skills and deep knowledge in different areas. Many provide formal mechanisms for assessing that knowledge, in a process known as prior learning assessment (PLA). This process allows students to document mastery of skills comparable to what they would learn in a university class and to obtain university credit for that knowledge.

The practice of awarding academic credit for prior learning has been widely adopted over the last few years by adult-serving universities, including large and small institutions, and both nonprofit and for-profit schools.[29] Some states, such as Ohio, Montana, Texas, Wisconsin, New York, and Tennessee, have created guidelines and implemented PLA across multiple public universities.[30]

Several processes are used for PLA. Mastery can be documented by taking nationally standardized exams, such as the College Level Examination Program (CLEP) and the Defense Activity for Non-Traditional Education Support (DANTES) tests. In addition, many universities offer exams created by academic departments to demonstrate mastery.[31]

In addition to testing, universities can award credit based on military training, courses, or experiences; guidelines for awarding academic credit have been developed by the American Council on Education (ACE).[32]

A third approach is through assessment of portfolios that demonstrate mastery. The Council for Adult and Experiential Learning (CAEL) provides an electronic platform to support portfolios, training for assessors, and also assessment services by their own experienced and trained assessors.[33] Research has found that adult students who receive credit for prior learning are more than twice as likely to complete either an associate or bachelor degree than are those who do not receive such credit.[34]

Massive Open Online Courses (MOOCs) and
MOOC-Based Graduate Programs

Another higher-educational product developed with growing frequency over the past ten years is the MOOC. There are two types: "cMOOCs," which do not involve grades and are essentially platforms for people to collaboratively explore a topic, and "xMOOCs," which involve assessment and are designed as large-scale online classes, meant to educate those who do not already have expertise. Very few cMOOCs exist; the overwhelming growth has been in xMOOCs.

MOOCs are classes developed by university professors who are experts in their fields. They include videos of lectures, usually in small chunks, interspersed with assessments such as multiple-choice tests and applied projects, generally graded by other students in the course using a fixed rubric. Most involve asynchronous discussion by students, some led by professors and teaching assistants, and others offered without facilitation. By some estimates there are now more than 2,500 MOOCs available, and they have taught tens of millions of students around the world.[35] Some estimates are even larger, describing 3,800 MOOCs offered or planned.[36]

There are several key features that make MOOCs radical innovations. First, they are open to all; there are no prerequisites, no enrollment requirements, and no matriculation is needed. They are generally free to take, although some providers offer the option of paying a small fee to have one's work graded by experts. Some are offered during a specific time frame, but most are available to begin at any time, disassociated from the academic (or any) calendar.[37]

Providers range from for-profit organizations that focus all their efforts on MOOCs, such as Coursera and Udacity, to nonprofit organizations such as edX. Other providers include learning management system vendors, such as Blackboard and Canvas. Some MOOCs provide a certificate of completion, but none provide direct academic credit. MOOCs allow anyone around the world to develop skill in nearly any field, for free. Some challenges, however, include (1) potential lack of academic integrity in assessment because there are no controls for cheating; (2) lack of online community; and (3) very high dropout rates.

In another innovation, some universities have used MOOCs as resources, combined with face-to-face meetings in a traditional class structure. Several of these experiments have been extremely successful, sharply increasing student success when compared with traditional courses.[38] In addition, a few traditional universities such as the University of Illinois and the Georgia Institute of Technology have collaborated with MOOC providers to select or develop a set of MOOCs that together form an online academic program; examples include a master of business administration, master of computer science in data analytics, and master of science in computer science degree programs.[39]

In these programs, students pay the host university, which hires professors to teach using the MOOC courses. Students participate in asynchronous and synchronous discussions, may work in teams, and are actively instructed by experts. These programs can be offered at large scale and very low cost, such as less than $8,000 for a master's degree.[40]

Boot Camps, Badges, and Micro-Credentials

Another higher-educational innovation, even farther removed from traditional university education, is the development of badges and micro-credentials. These involve mastery of skill sets at a different scale than the traditional associate's, bachelor's, and master's degrees; that is, awarding credential for learning that may be smaller than a course or beyond the scope of a bachelor's degree.

Badges represent mastery of skills at a smaller scale than a university course; for example, students may be awarded five or ten badges within the framework of a course.[41] Some badges are options within traditional university courses, whereas others are free standing. All badges are awarded online, for skills or knowledge demonstrated in an online setting. They are directed at a wide variety of ages, from K–12 to college and professional skills.

Because of this variety in the level of badges, there is no standard for the amount or level of complexity of learning represented by a badge; it can represent one or two skills or a large number of skills.[42] Many different vendors have created platforms for displaying digital badges, but they do not share information, so badges awarded in one platform cannot be recognized by other platforms.[43]

Micro-credentials provide mastery of skills and abilities at a larger scale than a course, but less than a master's degree. They include "Nano-degrees" offered by the MOOC provider Udacity,[44] and "Micro-masters" offered by another MOOC provider, edX.[45] Most of these degrees take between six months and a year to complete and involve anywhere from two to five MOOC-type courses of learning.[46]

These programs are aimed at professional employment, with titles ranging from Project Management to Virtual Reality Developer. They typically charge less than $2,000, and some far less if the cost of the courses are paid by employers who use them as recruiting venues. When used to recruit, employers subsidize the cost of instruction and reach out to high-performing students with job offers. Providers award successful students a certificate of completion rather than academic credit, and each micro-credential represents a different amount of learning and degree of skill.

A large number of private, for-profit organizations have developed "boot camps," primarily to teach different kinds of computer coding skills. These programs can range from one day to ten months, and prices range from less than $100 to $15,000.[47] All involve intensive study, with a five-day per week work, and are led by skilled expert instructors. Some are offered completely online,[48] whereas others involve face-to-face instruction.

These boot camps do not carry academic credit but do award certificates of completion. Because they are focused on a specific skill set, students can develop great proficiency in a narrow area. Because the time frames and intensity varies, the level of skill varies across boot-camp providers.

Another innovation is private for-profit firms that offer inexpensive online courses in general education areas such as English composition and world history. These courses do not carry academic credit but rather have been approved for credit by the American Council on Education. One such company is StraighterLine,[49] which has agreements with about one hundred universities to accept their courses for transfer credits.

The courses cost less than a hundred dollars to take and are developed by freelance academics, together with the academic publisher McGraw-Hill. The academic quality of the course materials varies, as does the level of support available from academically trained instructors; more support involves a higher cost.[50] The company has grown significantly over the past eight years and has developed multiple support options to meet the needs of a wide range of students, which has the potential to sharply decrease the costs of a degree for students in partner universities.[51]

Summary of Innovations

The innovations described appeal to different types of students and have different cost structures; a summary is shown in table 2.1.

EFFECT OF HIGHER-EDUCATIONAL CHANGES ON UNIVERSITY BUSINESS MODELS

The higher-education industry has seen enormous upheaval since the turn of the millennium. From 2000 to 2010, for-profit online universities arose and grew significantly. All of the innovative options and higher-educational products described previously have created much more competition for an increasingly expensive service. There are growing legislative pressures to reduce the cost of higher education, such as state regulations passed or pending in Ohio, Florida, Wisconsin,[52] Idaho, and Texas[53]

Table 2.1. Innovative Higher Educational Products, Markets, and Costs

Innovative Higher Educational Product	Type of Student	Cost Implications
Online Courses and Programs from Traditional Universities	Traditional, New Majority	Expensive—generally higher than traditional education.
Competency-Based Education (CBE)	New Majority	Very inexpensive to moderate, depending on requirement to complete courses
Prior Learning Assessment (PLA)	New Majority	Very inexpensive
MOOCs	Traditional, New Majority	Very inexpensive
MOOC-Based Graduate Programs	Traditional, New Majority	Moderate
Boot camps	New Majority	Moderate to expensive, depending on timeline
Badges	Traditional, New Majority	Inexpensive to expensive, depending on context and provider.
Micro-credentials	New Majority	Inexpensive to moderate, depending on provider

to force public universities to freeze tuitions.[54] One state even considered legislation requiring universities to pay for students' textbooks.[55]

The number of online courses offered by traditional universities has consistently grown over the past ten years. This does not reduce costs because a recent study found that online courses offered by universities tend to be slightly more expensive than face-to-face courses.[56]

The number of students enrolled in colleges or universities has declined every term since 2012.[57] Many universities are struggling, and according to the US Department of Education, 9,118 US-based college branches or locations closed their doors between 1998 and January of 2017; the rate has been growing since 2002.[58]

Because of all of these factors, the higher-educational landscape is in the midst of a major shift, and universities must respond with new models and approaches. Some institutions are creating "innovations centers" to support enhanced teaching practices[59] and expanding online learning offerings. However, these approaches use the traditional craft-based model of higher education in the design of courses,[60] wherein faculty are the experts who dedicate great time and energy in crafting each unique course. Innovations are seldom extended beyond individual faculty or courses, and faculty chooses entirely how to design courses.

Alternative ways to approach the work of developing and delivering educational products abound, all of which require moving away from the traditional craft model. The four elements of a business model include (1) the value proposition, or the outcome provided by an organization to its customers; (2) resources used, including people, technology, and facilities; (3) the processes used to transform inputs into outputs for customers, including all aspects such as budgeting, planning, and production; and (4) the profit formula, including all costs and revenues.[61] All of these elements must fit together for an organization to be successful, whether the organization is a university or auto manufacturer.[62]

Given declining demand for university education because of greater choices among educational products and increasing pressures to lower costs, recent analyses recommend that universities revise their business models in different ways.[63] Some examples include centralizing aspects of course development and delivery, as well as increasing standardization of course development and teaching practices and sharing and outsourcing resources.[64] These approaches move toward mass-production models, which reduce costs but can also reduce the quality of instruction.

As the number of students declines and educational costs rise, universities must develop innovative approaches that are flexible and student-focused and meet the needs of New Majority students. Educational offerings must include less-expensive options and must provide flexibility about time and place. Programs must be offered at different scales to fit into students' changing lives and requirements.

MOOC-based programs, badges, micro-credentials, PLA, and CBE all meet these requirements. Partnerships with low-cost course providers and development of intelligent systems that provide customized learning pathways and feedback at very low cost also meet these needs. Merely moving courses and programs online but maintaining the same time frame, cost structure, academic roles, and rigid program design is not enough. The structures and processes used must match the products that are offered, the value proposition and the costs, to enable success. This requires new approaches to the design and delivery of higher education.

KEY POINTS

- Traditionally universities have offered a "bundled" product that included academics, a residential experience, research, and extra-curricular programming along with a credential. Some view the traditional university as providing a safe place to grow up for emerging young adults.
- The educational market has become much more competitive, with the rise of nonprofit, online programming, and alternative credentialing models. These market forces are pressuring universities to "unbundle" the university product.
- Unbundled products are attractive to New Majority students, who may not seek a residential experience and may not be able to afford educational "amenities." To thrive in this emerging marketplace, institutions will need to find more efficient ways of producing and delivering the educational products that will continue to be demanded by New Majority students.

NOTES

1. C. Adelman, P. Ewell, P. Gaston, and C. Geary Schneider, *The Degree Qualification Profile* (Indianapolis, IN: Lumina Foundation, 2014), https://www.luminafoundation.org/files/resources/dqp.pdf.

2. Adelman et al., *The Degree Qualifications Profile*.

3. L. Armstrong, "Cost Allocation in the Research University and What It Tells Us," *Changing Higher Education*, March 2, 2015, http://www.changinghighereducation.com/2015/03/cost-allocation-in-the-research-university.html.

4. T. Umbach, *The Economic and Societal Impact of the University of Minnesota*, http://impact.umn.edu/assets/pdf/Final_Report.pdf.

5. Internet Live Stats, "United States Internet Users," http://www.internetlivestats.com/internet-users/us.

6. O. Petitte, "Infographic Shows $13 Billion Spent Worldwide on MMOs in 2012," *PC Gamer*, December 15, 2012, http://www.pcgamer.com/mmo-infographic.

7. Statista: The Statistics Portal, "Number of Monthly Active Facebook Users Worldwide as of Fourth Quarter 2016," https://www.statista.com/statistics/264810/number-of-monthly-active-facebook-users-worldwide.

8. M. Mitchell, M. Leachman, and K. Masterson, "Funding Up, Tuition Down: Funding Cuts to Higher Education Threaten Quality and Affordability at Public Colleges," Center on Budget and Policy Priorities, August 15, 2016, http://www.cbpp.org/research/state-budget-and-tax/funding-down-tuition-up.

9. N. Tafuri, "Prices of US and Foreign Published Materials, 2016," American Library Association Institutional Repository, https://alair.ala.org/handle/11213/7524.

10. Tafuri, "Prices of US and Foreign Published Materials."

11. University Library, University of Illinois at Urbana-Champaign, "The Cost of Journals," http://www.library.illinois.edu/scholcomm/journalcosts.html.

12. The Davis Educational Foundation, "An Inquiry into the Rising Cost of Higher Education: Summary of Responses from 70 College and University Presidents," http://www.davisfoundations.org.

13. S. Quinton, "The High Cost of Higher Education," Stateline, The Pew Charitable Trusts, January 25, 2016, http://www.pewtrusts.org/en/research-and-analysis/blogs/stateline/2016/01/25/the-high-cost-of-higher-education.

14. M. Michell and M. Leachman, "Years of Cuts Threaten to Put College Out of Reach for More Students," Center on Budget and Policy Priorities, May 13, 2015, http://www.cbpp.org/research/state-budget-and-tax/years-of-cuts-threaten-to-put-college-out-of-reach-for-more-students.

15. American Academy of Arts and Sciences, "Public Research Universities: Changes in State Funding," https://www.amacad.org/multimedia/pdfs/publications/researchpapersmonographs/PublicResearchUniv_ChangesInStateFunding.pdf.

16. Mitchell, Leachman, and Masterson, "Funding Up, Tuition Down."

17. Mitchell, Leachman, and Masterson, "Funding Up, Tuition Down."

18. A. Jahnke, "Who Picks Up the Tab for Science?" *BU Research*, http://www.bu.edu/research/articles/funding-for-scientific-research.

19. I. E. Allen and J. Seaman, "Grade Level: Tracking Online Education in the United States," Babson Survey Research Group and Quahog Research Group, 2015, http://www.babson.edu/Academics/faculty/provost/Pages/babson-survey-research-group.aspx.

20. I. E. Allen and J. Seaman, "Online Report Card: Tracking Online Education in the United States," Babson Survey Research Group and Quahog Research Group, 2016, http://www.babson.edu/Academics/faculty/provost/Pages/babson-survey-research-group.aspx.

21. J. Leafstead and M. Pacansky-Brock, "Faculty Development in the Age of Digital, Connected Learning," *EdSurge News*, December 15, 2016, https://www.edsurge.com/news/2016-12-15-faculty-development-in-the-age-of-digital-connected-learning.

22. P. Hill, "Online Program Management: An Updated View of the Market Landscape," *eLiterate*, September 8, 2016. Accessed February 20, 2017, from http://mfeldstein.com/online-program-management-updated-view-market-landscape

23. R. Kelchen, "The Landscape of Competency-Based Education: Enrollments, Demographics and Affordability," Center on Higher Education Reform, American Enterprise Institute, 2015, http://www.aei.org/publication/landscape-competency-based-education-enrollments-demographics-affordability.

24. Western Governors University, "WGU Timeline," http://www.wgu.edu/about_WGU/timeline.

25. Kelchen, "The Landscape of Competency-Based Education."

26. S. Jaschik, "Evaporating Fears on Competency-Based Education," *Inside Higher Education*, January 30, 2017, https://www.insidehighered.com/digital-learning/article/2017/01/30/provosts-no-longer-fear-impact-competency-based-education.

27. http://degreeprofile.org.

28. Educational Testing Service, "ETS Proficiency Profile," https://www.ets.org/proficiencyprofile/about.

29. R. Klein-Collins and J. N. Wertheim, "The Growing Importance of Prior Learning Assessment in the Degree Completion Toolkit," *New Directions in Adult and Continuing Education*, Winter 2013.

30. Council for Adult and Experiential Learning, "State System PLA Adoption: Lessons from a Three-System Initiative," https://www.cael.org/pla/publication/state-system-pla-adoption-lessons-from-a-three-system-initiative.

31. Ohio Board of Regents, *PLA with a Purpose: Prior Learning Assessment and Ohio's College Completion Agenda*, https://www.ohiohighered.org/sites/ohiohighered.org/files/uploads/PLA/PLA-with-a-Purpose_Report_FINAL_041614_0.pdf.

32. Ohio Board of Regents, *PLA with a Purpose*.

33. Council of Adult and Experiential Learning, http://www.cael.org.

34. R. Klein-Collins, *Fueling the Race to Postsecondary Success: A 48-Institution Study of Prior Learning Assessment and Adult Student Outcomes* (Council for Adult and Experiential Learning, 2010), http://www.cael.org/pdfs/PLA_Fueling-the-Race.

35. R. Schroeder, "Online: Trending Now #100—What Have We Learned So Far?" University Professional and Continuing Education Association, http://upcea.edu/online-trending-now.

36. E. Wexler, "MOOCs Are Still Rising, at Least in Numbers," *Wired Campus* (blog), *Chronicle of Higher Education*, October 19, 2015, https://www.chronicle.com/blogs/wiredcampus/moocs-are-still-rising-at-least-in-numbers/57527.

37. J. R. Young, "Are MOOCs Forever?" *Chronicle of Higher Education*, July 14, 2016, http://www.chronicle.com/article/Are-MOOCs-Forever-/237130.

38. F. M. Hollands and D. Tirthali, *MOOCs: Expectations and Reality*, Center for Cost-Benefit Studies of Education, Teachers College, Columbia University, http://cbcse.org/wordpress/wp-content/uploads/2014/05/MOOCs_Expectations_and_Reality.pdf.

39. J. Friedman, "MOOC-Based Credential Options Expand in Online Education," *US News and World Report*, October 6, 2016. http://www.usnews.com/education/online-education/articles/2016-10-06/mooc-based-credential-options-expand-in-online-education.

40. Online Master of Science, Computer Science, Georgia Institute of Technology, http://omscs.gatech.edu/home.

41. J. Friedman, "Online Courses Experiment with Digital Badges," *US News & World Report*, December 10, 2014, https://www.usnews.com/education/online-education/articles/2014/12/10/online-courses-experiment-with-digital-badges.

42. Digital Badges, MacArthur Foundation, https://www.macfound.org/programs/digital-badges.

43. M. J. Madda, "How to Make Micro-Credentials Matter," *EdSurge News*, February 2, 2015, https://www.edsurge.com/news/2015-02-02-how-to-make-micro-credentials-matter.

44. Nanodegree, Udacity, https://www.udacity.com/nanodegree.

45. Micromasters, edX, https://www.edx.org/micromasters.

46. Friedman, "MOOC-Based Credential Options Expand in Online Education."

47. A. Williams, "Coding Bootcamp vs. Self-Study," *Course Report*, October 1, 2015, https://www.coursereport.com/blog/bootcamp-vs-self-study-the-complete-guide.

48. One-Day Boot Camps, Learning Tree International, https://www5.learningtree.com/info/bootcamp-courses.htm.

49. StraighterLine, http://www.straighterline.com.

50. S. Golden, "A Curricular Innovation, Examined," *Inside Higher Ed*, December 16, 2010, https://www.insidehighered.com/news/2010/12/16/review_of_straighterline_online_courses.

51. L. Alexander, "An Update on StraighterLine—A Disrupter in the Making?" *Changing Higher Education*, January 26, 2015, http://www.changinghighereducation.com/2015/01/straighterline.html.

52. K. Herzog, "UW Regents Extend Tuition Freeze," *Milwaukee Journal-Sentinal*, October 7, 2016, http://www.jsonline.com/story/news/education/2016/10/07/uw-regents-take-back-tuition-setting/91727382.

53. L. McGaughy, "Key Senator Pitches Four-Year Tuition Freeze at Texas Public Colleges." *Dallas Morning News*, January 19, 2017, http://www.dallasnews.com/news/

higher-education/2017/01/19/key-senator-pitches-four-year-freeze-texas-college-tuition.

54. Quinton, "The High Cost of Higher Education."

55. K. Farkas, "Tuition Freeze at Ohio Public Colleges Would Continue under Gov. Kasich's Budget," *Cleveland.com*, January 30, 2017, http://www.cleveland.com/metro/index.ssf/2017/01/kasich_again_proposes_tuition.html.

56. R. Poulin and T. T. Straudt, *Distance Education Price and Cost Report* (WICHE Cooperative for Educational Technologies [WCET], February 2017), http://wcet.wiche.edu/sites/default/files/Price-and-Cost-Report-2017_0.pdf.

57. P. Fain, "National College Enrollments Continue to Slide," *Inside Higher Ed*, December 19, 2016, https://www.insidehighered.com/quicktakes/2016/12/19/national-college-enrollments-continue-slide.

58. Federal Student Aid, US Department of Education, "Closed School Weekly/Monthly Reports," https://www2.ed.gov/offices/OSFAP/PEPS/closedschools.html.

59. D. Raths, "How to Launch a Campus Innovation Center," *Campus Technology*, February 17, 2016, https://campustechnology.com/Articles/2016/02/17/How-to-Launch-a-Campus-Innovation-Center.aspx.

60. B. Rubin, "University Business Models and Online Practices: A Third Way," *Online Journal of Distance Learning Administration* 16, no. 1 (2013), http://www.westga.edu/~distance/ojdla.

61. C. Christensen, M. Horn, L. Caldera, and L. Soares, *Disrupting College: How Disruptive Innovation Can Deliver Quality and Affordability to Postsecondary Education* (Center for American Progress, 2011), https://www.americanprogress.org/issues/economy/reports/2011/02/08/9034/disrupting-college.

62. L. Alexander, "A Business Model View of Changing Times in Higher Education," *Changing Higher Education*, December 12, 2014, http://www.changinghighereducation.com/2014/12/new_business_model_view_of_change_in_higher_education.html#more.

63. Rubin, "University Business Models and Online Practices."

64. Poulin and Straudt, *Distance Education Price and Cost Report*.

THREE

Defining Your University Product

Eric Malm

IT ALL STARTS WITH "RE"

The letters *re* can be surprisingly scary or exciting. Redesign. Reimagine. Restructure. For some, the opportunity to redesign something is an opportunity for creative discovery. For others, the thought of restructuring a program or department brings with it the threats of change: new responsibilities, new objectives, and new power dynamics. Change can be a two-edged sword.

In the *Harvard Business Review* article, "Reinventing Your Business Model," authors Johnson, Christensen, and Kagermann argue that even big, successful companies should periodically examine what they do and search for opportunities in reinvention.[1] One piece of their framework is the customer value proposition, or the reasons why customers buy and value a company's product. The process of examining the customer value proposition can clarify what a company does and shed light on opportunities for improvement. The process of reimagining and reinventing is as appropriate for higher education as it is for the manufacturing or financial-services industries.

In this chapter a framework is presented that stakeholders from across a higher-education institution can use to help talk about what an institution "produces" and how it generates value for its customers. On the surface, the product of higher education is fairly simple; universities produce educated students and expand the base of knowledge, among other things. But as we'll see, the ideas of product and customer value are much richer and more complicated.

COMPETITIVE SPACES AND PEER INSTITUTIONS

Most institutions keep a list of "peer" and "aspirant" institutions. Students conducting a college search can typically identify the important (and unimportant) attributes that they are looking for, and translate that into a list of similar schools. But the universe of colleges and universities is immense. The increasing number of online programs that institutions offer represent both opportunity and threat. Institutions may draw new students into online and hybrid programs, but they are also forced to compete with a broader set of schools and program types.[2] So as we begin to reimagine and redesign our programs, it's important that stakeholders can articulate what it is that a particular school does well.

Institutions span many dimensions. What is the average SAT score of students? What is the tuition? Does the school have top-notch athletic teams? Nationally recognized researchers? Well-equipped labs? An active campus social environment? Clearly many different attributes are important. William Massey characterizes the "value proposition" of traditional undergraduate programs as including the following:[3]

- value-added education for career and life,
- credentials,
- relationships and diversity,
- socialization and consumption, and
- a "taste of greatness."

Each institution, of course, offers students a different combination of experiences and appeals to different types of students at different price points. Although online programs will likely focus almost exclusively on career education and relevant credentials, residential programs offer more varied (and costlier) student experiences.

Defining how an institution provides value to students is increasingly important. Although universities are sometimes described as being in an "arms race" to build better facilities, luxurious dorms, and high-end dining halls, and fund costly athletic teams, each institution must offer a combination of features that caters to the needs and profiles of incoming students, uses available resources, and fits with the university's financial constraints.

Figure 3.1 illustrates how an institution's academic or "learning," product emerges from a broader institutional context. In the same way that athletics, residence life, and admissions must all work to efficiently provide student services, the academic side of the house must also work to continually update how the student learning product is being produced. Although institutions clearly have many products, the remainder of this chapter will focus on the institution's learning or academic products. For example, one institution may offer advanced study in very specific subject areas, whereas another institution's mission may be to provide affordable education to a broad range of students or to meet the needs of a targeted type of learner.

THE LEARNING PRODUCT: AN ECONOMIST'S PERSPECTIVE

This book is about how to redesign and restructure programs and services to better meet the needs of New Majority learners. This means we need to think both about what types of services today's learners need (what programs we provide), and how they are "produced" (how students learn). As we think about change in academia, it can be helpful to think about how economists model production and change in other industries.

Economists typically say that firms use different inputs (such as labor and capital) to produce their output. For example, a bakery needs to decide on what combination of workers and equipment to use to make donuts. One bakery may mix dough using a mechanical mixer, whereas another bakery may mix ingredients by hand using spoons and a bowl. The objective of the bakery is to make donuts, and hiring bakers or buying mixing equipment is done for the purpose of making donuts. Bakeries are also in a constant process of adaptation and change. Over time bakeries may find that market conditions have changed, and healthier muffins are preferred to cream-filled donuts, so they change the quantity of each they produce each day. Or they may find that prices or technology have changed, and it may make sense to use a machine to do some-

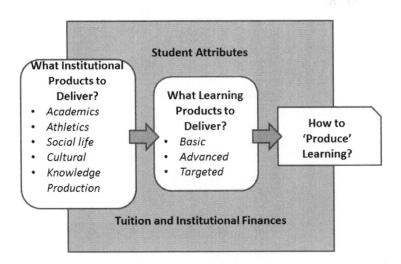

Figure 3.1. The Learning Product in an Institutional Context

thing that was once done by a person. These same concepts apply to academic institutions.

Product, Productivity, and Learning

We started this chapter by discussing the various products of the university and then focused more specifically on the academic or learning product. A core issue is how we measure the academic product of higher education. Although we won't come to any clear, universally agreed-on quantitative measures here, the primary goal is to talk about the issue and consider a variety of possible ways to measure the product of higher education. At the institutional level, we commonly talk about retention rates, NSSE (National Survey of Student Engagement) scores, graduation rates, and job placement rates. Clearly these are all measures of output or product.

At the other end of the spectrum, we also view enrolled students, or bodies in seats, as another measure of output. More recently the federal government has pushed this measure a bit further, insisting that the student needs to complete the course for financial aid to be fully received by the institution.[4] All of these measures have value, yet none perfectly measures output or learning.

Set aside the complications of measuring learning for a moment. We can all imagine certain course formats or structures that are more effective than others. A student may be able to learn a certain amount by reading a book in isolation. But interaction with other students, the opportunity to see and apply concepts in the real world, and insight and feedback from an instructor can clearly result in more learning than would occur from reading a book in isolation. If one accepts that there's a relationship between the educational inputs (as an economist might call things like the instructor, students, active learning experiences, etc.) and output or learning, then it's easy to accept the proposition that there's a relationship between cost (expended by the institution) and learning (acquired by the student).

Now let's apply a standard economic model to education. If the quantity of donuts produced is a function of the number of bakers in various roles, ovens, kitchen equipment, and ingredients then we can similarly think of the amount of learning produced as being influenced by the number and quality of teachers, the availability of support staff, the appropriate use of technology, and a host of other factors. We can formalize this in a simple economic model:

$$\text{Student Learning (or "Output")} = f(\text{labor, technology, support services, format, other factors})$$

Where *student learning* is a function of

I = instructors
EC = nonfaculty educational collaborators[5]
S = support staff
T = technology
F = format
C = cohort of fellow students

In the discipline of economics, we balance productivity and cost. When a bakery manager is faced with the decision of whether to use more workers or more machines to increase donut output, he or she will consider both the marginal product of labor and capital as well as their respective prices. The *marginal factor rule* says that a bakery manager should hire the factor of production with the highest marginal productivity per dollar. When faced with the need to increase output, the bakery manager would consider how many more donuts an additional worker (or machine) would produce, along with the cost of hiring the worker (or machine).

Economists also stress that the productivity of a worker relies on other inputs. In higher education, we must consider both the contribution of various factors to student learning as well as the cost of these factors. We must also recognize, for example, that the productivity of teachers depends on the amount of technology at their disposal, the availability of support resources, and so on.

Resources, Trade-offs, and Learning

Cost is sometimes viewed as an unseemly subject in higher education. Teachers would like to have more resources available to help their students learn and succeed, yet budgets are always tight. And every student would like it if their tuition bill wasn't quite so high. But as with any business, higher education needs to have more conversations about cost, accountability, and the tough choices that colleges and universities will continue to need to make regarding how resources are allocated throughout the enterprise.

For example, a university could offer one large online section of microeconomics each year, with one hundred students, in place of four face-to-face classes of twenty-five each or five classes of twenty. Decisions about class size and format are often made at the department or divisional level based on what is appropriate for different courses. One could argue that the small face-to-face class should always deliver more learning per student than a large online class, but institutions may (in good conscience) decide to offer a larger online class, knowing that it delivers less *learning per student* but has a lower cost. The point is that universities currently do make decisions about how to best deliver an acceptable level of learning (rather than the most possible learning), given financial and other constraints.

Decisions about cost and learning don't just involve class size. For example, a statistics instructor may need to include writing assignments in a statistics course but may not feel that writing instruction is a strength. One possibility would be for a writing specialist to join the class, decreasing the amount of work required of the instructor (for writing instruction), but allowing the instructor to serve a slightly larger class. The additional tuition revenue could fund the cost of the writing instructor, and it's quite likely that the level of learning would increase. A comparison of the quality of writing before and after the addition of the writing specialist may show improved learning, yet the reformulated class may have comparable, or even better, financials.

To begin to apply this model, we can consider two hypothetical colleges or universities that could conform to "craft" and "mass-production" models of higher education that Rubin describes.[6] In the craft model of education, students and faculty interact in a fairly traditional way, primarily in a face-to-face mode, with high levels of student-faculty interaction. One could consider a well-endowed, highly selective college with an 8:1 student-to-faculty ratio as an example. In such an institution, with excellent facilities and abundant personal attention, one expects that significant learning will take place—but at a high cost.

In contrast, the mass-production model describes many for-profit institutions that deliver relatively low-cost online education to large numbers of students. In these largely online programs, adjunct instructors typically deliver predefined courses to large numbers of students; if one takes retention and graduation rates as proxies for learning, these institutions deliver significantly less learning per student, for significantly less cost.

Figure 3.2 illustrates how the craft and mass-production models might be mapped in cost-learning space. The craft model is depicted as conveying high levels of learning at high costs. The mass-production model portrays lower levels of learning at lower costs. Within this context, a question emerges as to whether it is possible to restructure courses or programs to deliver higher levels of learning at a lower cost. A challenge for both mass-production and craft institutions is whether there are ways to improve the cost effectiveness of learning, reducing the cost of learning for craft institutions or increasing the amount of learning for mass-production institutions. This cost-of-learning framework encourages stakeholders to explicitly think about the trade-offs between cost and the amount of learning.

Implicit in this framework are the ideas that costs do matter and that costs and formats do affect student learning. For administrators, faculty, and program designers this framework pushes an explicit discussion of more cost-effective (although not necessarily lower cost) ways of struc-

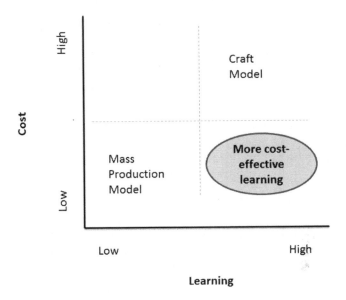

Figure 3.2. The Cost-of-Learning Framework

turing courses and programs. It should be noted that restructuring when, where, and how learning takes place often means replacing some resources with others (like replacing classrooms with online space or leveraging on-campus writing support services, for example). So within this context, it is important to discuss the role of shared resources.

THE ROLE OF SHARED COSTS

A particular challenge to university budgeting, and to measuring the true costs of learning, is that of shared costs. Universities have an enormous number of shared costs, from buildings and grounds, to the library, to academic support services and residence life staff. Additional students or a new program may place added burdens, for example, on the library.[7] Additional book titles or online subscriptions may need to be purchased, and the demand for library resources may expand. In university budgeting, it is fairly easy to identify specific resources (such as a periodical subscription) required to support a specific program, but many of these shared costs are much more difficult to observe.

In the zero-sum game of university budgeting, departments may be seen as competing for resources specific to their programming but are unlikely to want to contribute toward (or be billed for) the use or expansion of shared resources. According to economic theory, shared resources tend to be underprovided by the market.[8] In a university context, unless shared resources are paid for by those who use them, they will be chronically underfunded and understaffed. Because shared costs represent a significant percentage of university costs, these difficult conversations about shared resources need to be openly discussed.

DEFINING YOUR UNIVERSITY'S PRODUCT

Exploring a university's product and market can be a fun and useful exercise. One place to start is to ask stakeholders to place an institution within the cost-learning space (see figure 3.3). Where would people place their institution? Where would people place peer or aspirant institutions? It may also be useful to ask whether there are existing pressures within the institution to "move" within the cost-learning space. These discussions force participants to address cost and learning issues directly and can be a good segue into deeper conversations about institutional change.

Another useful group exercise is to ask groups of stakeholders from across an institution to begin to list important aspects and attributes of the institution's product. Table 3.1 shows results from a brainstorming session by students regarding a university's product.

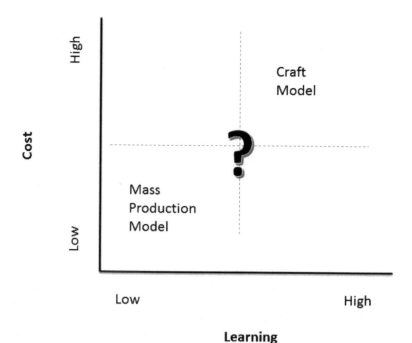

Figure 3.3. Placing Your Institution in a Cost-Learning Space

Table 3.1. Reasons for Choosing My University

Tuition/financial aid	Athletics	Professors
Campus location	Atmosphere	"I love the people
Small class size	Transfer credits	around here"

Table 3.2 shows results from a brainstorming session with students regarding the university's academic product. Similar brainstorming sessions could be held with stakeholders from across an institution (including faculty, students, and staff). There are no right or wrong answers for an institution, but it's important that people within an institution can generally agree on the institution's product, or value proposition.

Table 3.2 Academic Attributes

Small class size	Business program	Job connections
Professors know your name	Social justice aspect	Academic assistance and support
Internships	Experienced professors	

CHANGE MANAGEMENT AND LEADERSHIP

An underlying premise of this book is that higher-educational institutions need to change to better meet the needs of the students they have, but that this change can and should be consistent with their core strengths and educational missions. They say that the status quo requires no leadership, but change does. So for colleges and universities to change, leadership is required.

One model of change management asserts that change needs to start with a sense of dissatisfaction (D) with the present, which can then lead to a shared vision (V) of a possible future. First steps (F) toward that new state can be envisioned. But there is always resistance (R) to change, so the question is whether the product of dissatisfaction, vision, and the effort involved in taking first steps can outweigh institutional resistance.[9] This can be written in equation form as

$$D \times V \times F > R$$

One can argue that change is only possible if stakeholders sense a dissatisfaction with the present and share some sort of shared vision of a better future. Although a university's top administrative leaders can try to push for a specific vision of the future, the chances that this vision will be realized are much greater if there is grassroots buy-in from stakeholders across the institution. When a vision and reason for change comes from the stakeholder community, institutional resistance is lower and first steps become more easily imagined.[10]

Working from Within to Implement Change

Although driving change is often considered the role of academic leaders, university stakeholders should actively participate and support conversations about change even if those conversations are uncomfortable. By working from within, stakeholders can have a more active and empowered role in their institutional and professional futures. By proactively addressing change issues stakeholders can use their skills, knowledge, and experience to shape their futures. Although there is risk involved in suggesting change, the status quo brings with it the risk of more disruptive change.

Redesign, Trade-offs, and Resources

Figure 3.4 illustrates an innovation cycle for program redesign. Consider a program innovation for adult learners, such as the establishment of local study circles that would allow online students to meet with other students enrolled in the course at a local coffee shop to work together on class assignments. To implement such an idea, the school may need to provide an online tool that allows students to identify and schedule meeting places and times. In addition, the school may choose to partner with an organization (like Starbucks) and buy the students gift cards to pay for coffee. The institution may also need to provide faculty development to help create assignments that can be completed together in a coffee shop. Additional online resources may be required that students could access from the remote location. There are costs associated with all of these elements.

From a learning perspective, these coffee-shop projects may take the place of individual homework or online group work assignments. Leveraging peer-to-peer learning, active learning assignments, and the convenience of a local coffee shop, it is hoped that student learning may increase. A plan may be put in place to compare the work product of individual online assignments with those of coffee-shop projects to determine whether the new format improves learning outcomes.

The bottom line, so to speak, is to compare the financial costs and learning benefits of the innovation to determine the relative impacts on cost and learning. If an innovation has little cost and the potential to significantly increase learning, then it's probably worth doing! As with any innovation, adjustments are always necessary. The cycle provides for feedback and adjustment that can provide accountability and aid in budget and program-development discussions.

What happens if the innovation is successful? Each innovation should have explicit budget implications. Many times an innovation, such as the coffee-shop study circle described, may represent a shift in resources. Perhaps the study circle takes the place of a staffed recitation period, or

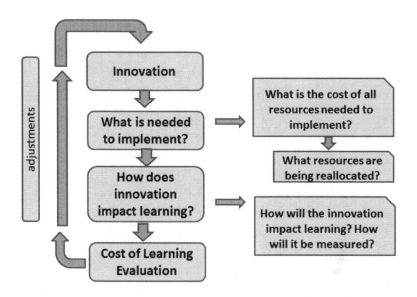

Figure 3.4. An Innovation Cycle for Program Design

frees up time for a faculty member to serve a slightly larger class. If this is the case, then these shifts should also be reflected in budgets.

Although some innovations can be adopted through existing budget processes, it may be desirable to have explicitly designated "innovation funds" available for new program testing. Because there is an implicit risk in losing funding for an existing program if an innovative new program is not successful, there will be a natural reluctance to experiment and innovate.

However, a separately designated innovation fund would reduce that risk. But such a fund needs to have strings attached. If the innovation reallocates resources to leverage shared university resources, then eventually budgets must be shifted to reflect that reallocation. If the innovation allows faculty to serve more students, then class-size caps need to increase. Not properly handled, innovation can lead to budget creep. But properly handled, an innovation fund can help institutions transform to meet changing needs and maintain good financial health for the institution.

AGENTS OF CHANGE

As we have seen thus far, the education marketplace is changing rapidly. New technologies and new market participants have changed the competitive space, and changing student attributes have impacted what academic and university products New Majority learners are looking for. As frightening as change can be, change happens. Stakeholders within colleges and universities need to decide whether to be actively involved in setting an institutional course or whether to be passively buffeted by the winds of change.

This chapter provided some tools and language that stakeholders can use to have these discussions about institutional change. It is important to note that these conversations should include stakeholders from across the institution—faculty, staff, students, alums, employers, and others. Although academic leadership is vital, so is the active participation of higher education's most valuable resource—it's people.

KEY POINTS

- With the increasing variety of traditional and nontraditional educational offerings, it is important for institutions and their stakeholders to clearly define the educational products they are offering to student–customers.
- University stakeholders should consider how their institution consciously positions itself in cost and learning dimensions. Such a discussion brings the trade-offs institutions face regarding cost, quality, and mission to the fore.
- Today a widening variety of partners are involved in educating our students. Technologists, instructional designers, learning-support specialists, and other educational partners play an increasingly important role in student education. The value of these resources needs to be acknowledged, in both human and financial terms.
- University leaders and stakeholders need to adapt policies that allow for experimentation and change, while minimizing risk.

NOTES

1. M. W. Johnson, C. M. Christensen, and H. Kagermann, "Reinventing Your Business Model," *Harvard Business Review*, December 2008, 50–59.

2. https://nces.ed.gov/datalab/powerstats/default.aspx.

3. W. F. Massey, *Reengineering the University: How to Be Mission Centered, Market Smart, and Margin Conscious* (Baltimore: Johns Hopkins University Press, 2017).

4. Michael Pugh, "Dropping Out Means Paying Back Financial Aid," *Fastweb*, January 4, 2013, http://www.fastweb.com/financial-aid/articles/dropping-out-means-paying-back-financial-aid.

5. For example, community partners in service-learning environments.

6. Beth Rubin, "University Business Models and Online Practices: A Third Way," *Online Journal of Distance and Learning Administration* 16, no. 1 (2013), http://www.westga.edu/~distance/ojdla/spring161/rubin.html.

7. Donna M. Desrochers and Steven Hurlburt, *Trends in College Spending 2011–2014: A Delta Data Update*, American Institutes for Research (2014), http://www.deltacostproject.org/sites/default/files/products/Delta%20Cost_Trends%20College%20Spending%202001-2011_071414_rev.pdf.

8. Garrett Hardin, "The Tragedy of the Commons," *Science* 162, no. 3859 (1968): 1243–48.

9. See the Beckhard-Harris change model, as summarized at https://www.wheel. ie/sites/default/files/Beckhard-Harris Change Model-DVF.pdf.

10. In the software-development world, the ideas of stakeholder buy-in are critical and translate into development methodologies such as agile development.

FOUR

Student-Centered Design

Marguerite Weber

Academic transformation means redesigning the student experience with learning for the purpose not only of improving learning and persistence outcomes but also institutional efficiency and effectiveness. Redesign teams rethink the roles of all members of the learning experience: administration, faculty, staff, and students.

At the heart, academic transformation is the conviction that we can use technology to reorganize and scale content delivery and to reimagine spaces for authentic practice and feedback systems. The success of this design-thinking approach, however, hinges on the capacities of students to demonstrate habits of highly skilled and highly self-directed learners. Without that resource, the systems are flawed.

This chapter centers on how to prepare learners to fully engage in a redesigned experience and on the institutional investments needed to build learners' abilities to set realistic and aspirational goals and to manage the resources needed to achieve them. The intention is to lay the groundwork for transformation implementation teams. Teams that are tasked with creating responsive designs typically engage faculty, administrators, and instructional-design staff and use a student-centered design approach to create learning environments in which New Majority learners will contribute and thrive.

APPLYING LEARNING THEORIES TO
STUDENT-CENTERED DESIGN

As discussed in more detail in chapter 7, design thinking manipulates three "levers": (1) *human effort* or what the students, faculty, and related staff can, will, and should do; (2) *technology* or what kinds of teaching, learning, and data-compilation tasks can be best done electronically; and (3) *investments* or the costs to keep the redesign stable, including the costs to students and the institution.

Good design improves students' learning and their satisfaction (both factors in student retention), but it also starts with ensuring that the students are well prepared to enter these reimagined spaces. Because adult learners and other members of the New Majority are early "flight risks"—their attrition rates are higher than those for traditional learners—design principles that promote persistence, resilience, and optimism can and should be incorporated at each touch point of the student experience, from inquiry through alumni participation.

Two learning theories that support these goals are self-efficacy and transformative learning. Self-efficacy helps to reimagine student roles and interactions. Transformative learning provides a framework for persistence and resilience and inspires a passion for an area of study.

Self-efficacy, Bandura explains, is informed by the notion that belief shapes motivation, attitudes, and actions.[1] The strongest contributor is a student's ability to apply prior successful experience to the new challenge. With no clear applicable precedent, the next strongest influence is relating to others' experiences. Finally, without other references, the learner will take a general "gut check" to get somatic clues to the likelihood of success. Self-efficacy determines willingness to commit to a course of action, risk tolerance, level of effort, and persistence when confronted with difficulties.

Engaging New Majority learners in identifying their beliefs about their capabilities makes redesigned experiences more productive. First, making authentic connections between the world of work and classroom learning is a resource multiplier (because of increased feeling of knowing). Second, their perception that their successful work and life experiences have given them valuable academic skills will affect the students' return-on-investment calculations (being more capable means they're taking less of a risk of failure). Thus, their shifted perceptions of the cost of investing their time, energy, and goodwill may well tip the scales toward goal attainment.

Well-designed learning experiences explicitly connect students to what they know to be true about themselves—their strengths and their challenges. This approach leads to undoing their feelings of powerlessness and increases their sense of control over their lives and their future, thus making their effort more efficient and their learning more persistent.

Building students' self-efficacy also makes faculty and staff effort more efficient because students will take more risks and will demonstrate less learned helplessness; they will be more likely to be accountable for independent effort and to take advantage of technology scaffolds.

Limits to self-efficacy also impact design. First, even with strong self-efficacy, students can't accomplish tasks beyond their abilities. (However, if the learning experience offers students something that they value highly, the more resilient, persistent students will find a way to earn that reward, even if they have low levels of relevant skills.) Next, if students don't value the learning outcomes, it doesn't matter if they have self-efficacy. They won't contribute effort because they don't perceive the return on investment. So, early onboarding experiences must be frank about communicating effort required and the relevant value of the endeavor.

To support student retention and completion, implementation teams should determine appropriate practices that promote self-efficacy and space them across admissions, matriculation, orientation, early learning experiences, and student support services, but the course or program redesign should consider incorporating these strategies:

- Begin with opportunities to inquire on how past experiences relate to the task at hand.
- Connect the power of their self-efficacy beliefs (how the task relates to a past success, how similar others have been successful, or the physical and emotional cues to emerging mastery) to the work needed to be successful. Substitute hollow cheers ("I know you can do it!") with substantive information ("I know these efforts work.").
- Remind students of the value of the work to increase motivation to persevere in the face of difficulties.

Transformative learning proposes that people go through profound changes as they reconcile the new learning with their prior knowledge and beliefs.[2] Because it describes an arc of students' growing engagement through content, process, and premise reflections, it provides a structure for aligning design approaches with each of these goals, thus refining faculty effort.

At the core of transformative-learning theory, which was developed by Jack Mezirow from his work with adults in informal-learning experiences, is the belief that as students fully engage in increasingly complex and personal learning tasks, they change. They certainly change in their understanding of the subject; but more importantly, they change in their fundamental beliefs about their own sense of power and self-direction, and thus, they become more capable of autonomous, self-directed critical inquiry.

Focusing student-development efforts on transforming students into emerging peers who identify themselves as representatives of the institution, "ambassadors" for the programs and services that have deeply engaged them, yields stronger persistence outcomes as well as efficiencies across the student experience.

Table 4.1 provides a transformative-learning framework for curriculum design. It was created as a tool for training course-redesign implementation teams for the University System of Maryland Course Redesign Initiative and adapted as a curricular sequencing tool at another public university.

The table provides a model for how learners grow into their identification with a field of study: acquire essential content knowledge; practice arranging and deploying that content to solve problems with the discipline; synthesize content and solution processes to appreciate the scope, depth, and beauty of a discipline; and finally, use high levels of mastery to engage in the questions that the discipline hasn't solved yet.

Transformative learning impacts design thinking for academic transformation because it forms a framework for organizing what is most efficiently accomplished with human effort and what can be most efficiently accomplished with technology. It also provides a means for discussing "cost" issues as more than cost of instruction or of technology but rather as an expenditure of effort.

STUDENT-CENTERED DESIGN AND RETURN ON INVESTMENTS

Students come to college with a disposition to invest money (for tuition and fees, books, transportation costs, child care, lost wages) for a future benefit. But they have more than money at risk; they also risk their sense of themselves (the social and emotional risks associated with looking stupid or being a failure). They invest their goodwill for the future benefits of increased autonomy, stability, and respect. If their money, sense of self, energies, and goodwill are mishandled, then they are attrition risks. Good design invests these efforts wisely.

Students' perceptions of the value of persisting are shaped by what's needed to realize the end reward. For example, failing a general education (content-centered) course may require a student to retake it. This doubles the cost of effort and tuition for the relatively low reward of satisfying an imposed requirement, and it damages their beliefs in their ability and desires to persist. Therefore, a "cost-responsive" approach to redesign is one that reduces incidences of the D, F, W, and I grades. Common course redesigns then are those that use the content for pre- and posttesting of discrete knowledge and collaborative work to practice efficient learning habits.

Similarly, when students form a strong commitment to a program of study (typically with second and third courses in a curricular sequence), they learn how the discipline makes meaning, and they become more

Table 4.1. Transformative Learning Framework for Curriculum Design

Content Reflections	Process Reflections	Process/Premise Reflections	Premise Reflections
Definitions from a Curricular Perspective			
"What, Who, and When": discrete facts the field has agreed on.	The *"How"*: how underlying systems impact each other to cause a reaction.	The *"Why"*: why the work is useful to explain certain sets of issues.	The *"Why Not"*: Why haven't the mysteries or inconsistencies been resolved.
Purpose			
Introductory awareness of key concepts related to the field.	Practice defining good thinking processes valued by the discipline.	Emerging mastery in solving new problems; relating the work to values.	Emerging readiness to join and continue the work of the field.
Examples of Related Curricular Tools			
Foundational reading	College-career exploration	Student-faculty research	Internships
Learning communities	Student-led cocurricular activities	Conference attendance	Self-directed studies
		Tutoring others	Capstone projects
Examples of Related Instructional Strategies			
Online materials with self-tests	Online collaborative learning	Experiential learning	Conference papers and presentations
Student presentations	Explanation assignments	Synthesizing assignments	Argumentation and persuasion assignments
Summarizing assignments		Guided research	
Common Redesign Approaches			
Hybrid course where online is content acquisition, and face-to-face is testing understanding and engaging with others	Online courses with opportunities for face-to-face cocurricular activities Linked courses (one online and one face-to-face or hybrid)	Hybrid where online is for reflection and application; face-to-face is for experiential learning and provocative discussion	Synchronous online conferences with face-to-face seminars and experiential learning

Source: M. Weber, "Design for Student Success: Lessons Learned, Continuous Improvements Needed," in *Proceedings of the 10th Annual National Symposium on Student Retention*, ed. S. Whalen (Norman: University of Oklahoma, 2014), 107–118.

efficient learners. This transformation lowers opportunity costs: faster time to graduation, more time to balance life responsibilities, faster time to a career, and so on.

Therefore, redesign work in the center two columns of the table focuses on students' practicing effective strategies to deploy knowledge and good thinking processes. "Learning with" and "learning to" pedagogies are appropriate, and technology can be used to provide a safe environment to practice emerging skills, to connect learners to one another, and to connect them with increasingly professional-grade resources rather than with testing them on concepts.

Finally, the ultimate value of a program of study is that learners feel the courses have prepared them to enter the field as near-peers. They've trained their minds, their habits, and their dispositions to use their learning to solve complex life problems, and they want to know that their voice is strong and welcome in the community of practitioners that they are joining. Therefore, learning at the end of a curricular sequence centers on entering that community through authentic work in the field, spirited critiques of the field's failures and limitations, and engaged experiments in applying new thinking and new energies to resolving those gaps.

Academic innovation can lower the costs (time, treasure, and goodwill) for students when it makes the learning accessible and when it also reinforces efficient learning behaviors and commitment to degree completion. When we choose academic innovations appropriate in each venue (face-to-face, student-directed learning engagement, online), we realize efficiencies by assigning the highest impact practices to the most high-touch (and thus high-cost) experiences.

Human effort is both the largest cost in the learning environment and the only producer of the revenue to meet those costs. Thus, expenditures for effort and technology are constrained not only by what resources are available but also by what the revenue producers (students, the community, donors, etc.) want and are willing to invest. It is, therefore, important to weigh the cost of the student effort and to consider student investment when we design the innovations needed to improve efficiency and effectiveness of learning experiences.

Seen through the student effort lens, we can remember that as students become more skilled and efficient, their investment is smarter (passing every class attempted, being able to be more full-time while balancing other priorities).

APPROACHES TO REDESIGNING THE STUDENT EXPERIENCE

Redesign starts with the hypothesis that a well-crafted teaching environment (content, pedagogy, and technology) will solve problems with institutional effectiveness outcomes (student learning, institutional expenditures, student persistence behaviors). The process involves rethinking human effort (faculty, support staff, and students), deploying appropriate technology, and measuring the results on the business case (outcomes, persistence, cost per student, faculty workload, etc.). Making redesign choices starts with analyzing the local problem to be solved.

Typically, design teams select a course or program of study for redesign because they want to solve these problems:

- Unsatisfactory levels of students' achieved learning outcomes (at the course level) and the persistence of their learning (at the program level).
- Unsatisfactory levels of students' persistence outcomes (D, F, W, and I grades at the course level) and subsequent enrollment (at the program level).
- Low student satisfaction with the learning environment: course availability, textbook costs, residency costs (transportation, parking, child care, time off work), levels of engagement with faculty and peers, quality of assessment, and relevance of academic work.
- Low faculty satisfaction with the learning environment: course drift, preparation for subsequent learning experiences, curricular sequencing, engagement with colleagues, opportunities for scholarship, and opportunities for college service.
- Impact on the institution: escalating program costs, facilities constraints, costs for technology, levels of student persistence/graduation, especially with underrepresented student cohorts.

When the problem or problems have been identified, the team develops a hypothesis of the best design balance (effort + technology + financial investment). The redesign stages themselves then test and refine this hypothesis. Reis[3] articulates these stages:

- *Awareness*: gathering data on the current state of learning outcomes (at the course and program levels), areas of student and faculty satisfaction and dissatisfaction, and costs.
- *Exploration*: familiarity with course redesign models and emerging issues within the discipline.
- *Adoption/early implementation*: pilot initial design model, assess outcomes and impacts, and redesign to improve efficiency and effectiveness.
- *Mature implementation*: Take the pilot to scale and build sustainability systems.
- *Growth*: Disseminate findings and adapt the process to subsequent courses.

Evaluating the impact of common course redesign models[4] provides a good starting place for examining academic transformation from the student perspective.

- *Supplemental: Retains the face-to-face effort, but supplements face-to-face content delivery with technology-based out-of-class interactions.* The goal is to keep costs flat while improving measured learning outcomes. This model can also control in and out of the classroom "drift." Through standardized online supplements and frames for face-to-face "scripts," this redesign process can maintain quality control across course sections, advising responsibilities, orientation activities, and so on. Implementation issues include consensus building around selection of materials[5] and faculty and staff development in strategies to connect the content to the supplemental experiences.[6]
- *Replacement: Alters the face-to-face environment by substituting nontraditional learning activities.* This approach uses technology-delivered content, online discussions, experiential learning, coaching sessions, and so on, to reduce costs or increase capacity while maintaining high levels of demonstrated learning outcomes. The replacement model is often an approach to "blended learning" or "flipped classrooms" that frees up faculty or staff time to concentrate on formative assessments and on creating learning experiences that require students to apply the content they acquire through the nontraditional environments.

  To implement this approach, the institution needs a clear definition of blended learning[7] and should consider launching several courses in a blended environment to ensure consistency of student preparation for the level of self-direction needed.[8] For student affairs, activities, like orientation, cocurricular skills development, career interest workshops, internship preparation, and so on, practitioners should consider using a common design approach across multiple units to bring coherence to the student experience and to build on students' lived experiences in navigating college support systems.

  Implementation issues associated with this model include professional development in pedagogies of engagement,[9] teaching and learning with technology, and assessment as learning.[10] Student services must be prepared to support self-directed learning, time management, and learning with technology.[11]
- *Emporium: Uses technology or technology with tutoring to replace most of the direct content delivery provided by faculty or staff.* Students are responsible for making time-on-task decisions needed to achieve outcomes. Faculty or staff roles likely will shift to focus on summative assessments of student learning against standards. This model can lower costs, increase capacity, control for quality drift, and if the design is continually refined based on learning outcomes, increase measured learning. Implementation issues include facilities planning,[12] consensus on outcomes standards, curricular sequencing, and equity in student access to technology.[13]

- *Buffet: Provides an array of learning opportunities.* Students make guided choices to engage in lectures, discussions, workshops, outside reading material, labs, study groups, videos, and so on. Progress may be managed through a learning contract or experiential learning portfolio. The model can increase capacity while keeping costs flat or reduce costs while keeping capacity flat. Implementation issues center mostly on consensus building on the nature of the resources to provide and on sustaining the currency of the resources.[14] In addition, students need support in help-seeking behaviors, time management, and learning with technology.[15]
- *Online Learning Design: Provides flexible, typically asynchronous access to learning experiences.* The primary design element is spacing, which considers where in the course to provide levels of flexibility in how to demonstrate learning, where and how to interact with struggling learners, and where to demand students to perform to standards. These choices depend on whether the purpose of the course is to expose students to new content, to provide opportunities for perfect practice in the discipline, or to provide opportunities to practice being a member of the discipline's academic community.

  If it is a foundational course in the discipline or in general education, then the purpose might be to have students acquire a content base as well as some habits of effective learners. Then, like a content-driven face-to-face class, the innovation focuses on mirroring students' learning processes (chunking, spacing, timing, and intentional recursiveness). The course might integrate some electronic face-to-face interactions, like conferences, videos, recorded feedback, and so on.

  A lower-division core course in the major might be more focused on beginning to think and behave like an expert in the field; for this kind of process-focused course, the chunks might be larger, and the recursiveness might take place in increasingly complex contexts. The course might integrate simulations and wicked problems that require applied content and good thinking.

  An upper-division core course in the discipline might be arranged to determine what students don't yet know or can't yet do and then coaching (either by the faculty or by high-functioning teams) in perfect practice of higher-order cognitive skills. An online capstone course, on the other hand, might be most efficiently conducted under the student's own leadership and direction, with the faculty serving as an authentic audience and senior colleague to promote the student's emerging leadership.

These course redesign models aren't prescriptive. Rather, they provide discussion points for an implementation team to consider the learning goals, the students' needs, New Majority learner access and pragmatic considerations, quality standards, and faculty strengths and talents.

THREATS TO STUDENT-CENTERED DESIGN

Higher education has long rued the situation of academic "silos" that don't communicate or collaborate for success in institutional goals. However, like the weather, we are more likely to complain about it than to change it. In a design environment, though, these disconnections can be fatal.

Redesign efforts are deployed when an aspect of the student experience lacks the level of success needed for the whole institution to be successful. If constrained to one issue (i.e., redesigning how the institution recruits and matriculates adult learners), failures in one area might simply manifest themselves in another area, often resulting in frustrations that degrade the efforts and best intentions of the design team and in wasted resources that compromise the institution's overall health. In short, if the student engagement, development, and learning experiences aren't essentially connected and coherent from the student perspective, they fail.

Another threat is making design and implementation decisions based solely on program cost. For example, institutions may implement fully online orientation programs because the costs of bringing students to campus, feeding them, and staffing workshops directly outweigh the perceived value of delivering content. However, conflating exposure to campus information with using onboarding experiences to strengthen students' commitment to persist may not be a wise design decision, especially for New Majority learners who may not have the familiarity with an academic environment needed to put that discrete content into a useful context for later use.

The choice should be informed by the best combination of student capacity to benefit (human effort) with institutional capacity to sustain the effort (the business case) and the technology should both reinforce student transformation and scale the effort.

At a community college concerned about student attrition as well as low staff satisfaction with the abilities of learners to navigate support systems, in consultation with this author, the design team decided on a supplemental model.[16] The content that had formed the basis of summer orientation was transformed into interactive class-based activities, and online materials were made available to first-year experience faculty, academic advisors, and student-support staff, who were provided with "scripts" to direct students to the materials on a just-in-time basis.[17]

A final design problem is allowing available or new technology to drive decisions. When a new technology is available, there is often a rush to use it without thinking through how the other areas need to be redesigned to make the most of the new resource. For example, leading a redesign project sponsored by ITHAKA and the University System of Maryland, this author experienced good success with online tools to support a range of high-failure courses for their traditional freshmen (i.e., My Math Lab, My Writing Lab, My Accounting Lab, etc.), but not by using these online tools as they were intended to be used.

In developing a summer bridge program as an alternative to placement testing, planners created a side-by-side test. One cohort had longer self-directed time to consume the online skills materials in reading, writing, numeracy, and information literacy. They could contact online guides, tutors, and mentors when they had difficulties. The other cohort had little self-directed time. Class time was spent delivering the content covering similar topics. When those students were in the lab, they completed the same portfolio assignments, but coaches were there to talk them through planning and execution processes (specific self-efficacy-focused interactions).[18]

The costs for the technology package and those for the coaching staff were comparable; however, the placement outcomes, student satisfaction, and matriculation yield in the second cohort were superior to the lab-centric design. The initiative realized gains by questioning initial assumptions that online is always the best and cheapest way to deliver content for this specific population of fragile learners, reasoning that human effort investment at the early transition stage would better prepare students to realize online efficiencies in later stages of the program.

Academic transformation is never a walk in the park. One of the biggest barriers is coming to agreement on what is the cause of the problem or paradox. Be prepared to demand and provide evidence to test every supposition. Access to and comfort with data can be another barrier, so make sure that there is a "data person" on the team. Next, have the will to transform all of the sections of the course or all of the types of student interactions (i.e., advising, orientation, career research), preferably in the same modality (face-to-face, hybrid, or online).

Although it's possible to have different models within offerings once the transformation is complete, at least for the pilot phase, consider choosing one design model to test. In the same vein, address whether full- and part-time faculty will have the same opportunities to express concerns and contribute talent and how they will have the same access to resources.

Remember that the initial design, the one the team decides to pilot, is inherently wrong. The first try is almost never the best solution. Starting with the assumption that the design is fundamentally wrong allows you to be open minded and curious throughout the pilot phase. Be like Thomas Edison. When he struggled with inventing the lightbulb, he said, "I have not failed. I've just found 10,000 ways that won't work." Remember that the design-thinking process moves from hypothesis to heuristic to algorithm. Let your pilot tell you what needs further refinement on its way to being a best practice.

Another barrier centers on a cultural resistance to sharing course outcomes. In academia, we are most accustomed to delivering polished presentations that celebrate great accomplishments and that deliver conclusions that can be generalized. With guidance and support across governance structures, designers engaged in academic transformation need to create a safe space for difficult and specific conversations about failure.

In the same vein, although we know the transformed experience will ultimately benefit students, be prepared for student resistance. Because the heart of academic transformation is changing human effort, the students will cry foul when they realize that they have responsibility for their own learning.

Finally, from the very beginning, be clear about how savings will be reinvested. The best approach is to make specific plans for reinvestment in the department that is taking the redesign risk. Faculty and departments aren't used to talking about costs of instruction, and there's almost an inherent belief that if there were more funds there would be more learning. Academic transformation challenges that belief, so make sure that the participants and the departments benefit from their openness to change and bravery.

STUDENT LEARNING: A MODEL FOR CHANGE

The primary goal of student-centered design is to make the learning more efficient and effective. But learning is inherently messy and difficult. Therefore, redesign teams rely on mental models that are informed by theories of learning and on adaptable best practices that provide general patterns for deploying effort, technology, and financial investments.

Efficiencies come from increasing students' abilities to engage in their own learning and increasing the value of the effort by ensuring that the learning is focused, timely, and relevant. Efficiencies also include reducing students' costs and investments of time, money, and personal risk.

And too, academic innovation reduces the costs of effort on the part of the faculty and staff. Smart use of design can free up time for the most satisfying parts of our job, which include showing what is important and beautiful about our subjects and programs, taking part in the formation of future colleagues in our field or ambassadors for our schools, and creating conditions for student growth and transformation.

But the institution itself can learn. Just as students become more capable, productive, and efficient learners, so too the institution itself learns from academic transformation efforts.

KEY POINTS

- When redesign effort is informed by self-efficacy and transformative learning, students' increased engagement and ability become resource multipliers in the learning environment.
- Student-centered design reimagines resources in terms of investments of the time, energy, and goodwill of students, faculty, and staff. Smart design conserves these resources through making strategic decisions about effort, technology, and financial resources.
- Academic transformation deploys effort, technology, and institutional resources to improve student success outcomes: higher levels of learning, productive persistence, credential attainment, and lifelong advocacy.
- Because this approach requires new forms of collaboration and new approaches to sharing the hard work of promoting student learning, threats to student-centered design include the institution's capacity to tolerate risks and a culture of impermeable boundaries around key functions (academic affairs, student affairs, business and finance affairs, etc.).

NOTES

1. A. Bandura, *Self-Efficacy: The Exercise of Control* (New York: W. H. Freeman, 1997), 3.

2. J. Mezirow and Associates, *Learning as Transformation* (San Francisco: Jossey-Bass, 2000).

3. R. Reis, "Blended Learning as Transformational Institutional Learning (Part 1)," *Tomorrow's Professor eNewsletter* 85, no. 3: 1357.

4. C. Twigg, http://www.thencat.org. See also C. A. Twigg, "Using Asynchronous Learning in Redesign: Reaching and Retaining the At-Risk Student," *Journal of Asynchronous Learning Networks* 13, no. 3 (2009): 147–55.

5. J. L. Hearne, A. B. Henkin, and J. R. Dee, "Enabling Initiative and Enterprise: Faculty-Led Course Redesign in a STEM Discipline," *Educational Research Quarterly* 35, no. 1 (2011): 33–62. See also N. D. Vaughn, "A Blended Community of Inquiry Approach: Linking Student Engagement and Course Redesign," *The Internet and Higher Education* 13, nos. 1/2 (2010): 60–65.

6. S. Eliason and C. L. Holmes, "A Course Redesign Project to Change Faculty Orientation toward Teaching," *Journal of the Scholarship of Teaching and Learning* 12, no. 1 (2012): 36–48.

7. R. Reis, "Blended Learning as Transformational Institutional Learning (Part 2)," *Tomorrow's Professor eNewsletter* 85, no. 4: 1358.

8. P. M. Turner, "Next Generation Course Redesign," *Change* (Nov./Dec. 2009): 11–16.

9. L. D. Fink, *Creating Significant Learning Experiences* (San Francisco: Jossey-Bass, 2003).

10. Twigg, http://www.thencat.org.

11. Vaughn, "A Blended Community of Inquiry Approach."

12. S. M Ross and G. R. Morrison, "Constructing a Deconstructed Campus: Instructional Design as Vital Bricks and Mortar," *Journal of Computers in Higher Education* 24 (2012): 119–31.

13. Vaughn, "A Blended Community of Inquiry Approach."

14. University System of Maryland, "Academic Transformation at the University System of Maryland: A USM Strategic Priority," http://www.usmd.edu/usm/academicaffairs/CIELT.

15. M. Weber, "Design for Student Success: Lessons Learned, Continuous Improvements Needed," in *Proceedings of the 10th Annual National Symposium on Student Retention*, ed. S. Whalen (Norman: University of Oklahoma, 2014), 107–18.

16. http://www.higherlearningdesign.com.

17. R. Lloyd, personal communication, 2017.

18. M. Weber and B. Schneller, "Theory of Bridges: Designs for Successful Student Transitions," Presentation at LiveText Conference on Assessment, July 2014.

FIVE

Efforts to Transform Learning: Rethinking Roles and Structures

William A. Egan, Marguerite Weber, and Eric Malm

So far, contributors have explored how the rapidly changing education marketplace has placed pressure on institutions to reimagine their university products and shown how student-centered design is critical for meeting the needs of New Majority learners. This chapter considers how two institutions restructured internal resources to create learning experiences that are both pedagogically and financially efficient.

Both Penn State University (PSU) and Cabrini University reimagined place, using technology to connect professors in real time with students in classrooms across multiple campus sites. From a student perspective, the PSU virtual-learning network (VLN) allowed adult students to engage in an in-the-classroom experience close to home. From an institutional perspective, the program is financially beneficial because it allows a single professor to be "present" in more than one place at the same time.

At Cabrini, an adult-education access pedagogy was created in which New Majority students took paired courses that included linked assignments. During a weekly in-person meeting with a learning mentor, students applied concepts learned in two different online classes and solved challenging, integrated problems. The format is designed to be time efficient for students. Because online faculty effort can be spread across multiple classrooms and mentors, the program restructures faculty costs as well.

REIMAGINING PLACE: THE PSU VLN

PSU was founded in 1855 and is the Commonwealth of Pennsylvania's largest public university. With the main campus in State College, PSU has twenty-four campus locations across the commonwealth; this also includes Penn State World Campus, which provides online and distance education programming. PSU offers approximately more than 160 baccalaureate- and graduate-degree programs and more than 90 associate-degree programs.[1]

In fall 2012, PSU expanded access through an initiative for a live interactive network of teaching and learning with the VLN, which allows campuses to share instruction through an interactive hybrid format. Through more than twenty high-technology classrooms equipped with high-definition video-conferencing technologies, learners participate in the same course at the same time with up to four campus locations via live video.[2] The goal of the VLN model was to help Pennsylvania adults acquire the learning needed to be competitive in the job market. VLN courses follow a hybrid model where the synchronous face-to-face and video-class sessions and online components complement one another to help reinforce course content and focus student learning.

VLN MBA Program

The Penn State Great Valley School of Graduate and Professional Studies, located just outside of Philadelphia in Malvern, offers master's degrees and graduate certificates in business, big data, engineering, finance, health care, leadership, and technology both online and on campus.[3] Through the VLN, Great Valley's AACSB-accredited MBA degree program was delivered to the Reading area at Penn State Berks, a residential and commuter campus specializing in two-year associate-degree and four-year bachelor-degree programs. The VLN MBA partnership provides Reading-area professionals a convenient way to continue their education with PSU.[4]

The MBA VLN program is an accelerated program where courses are offered in seven-week terms delivered in a hybrid format (a blend of online instruction coupled with the synchronous classroom sessions). Students meet one night a week for a three-hour synchronous class session either face-to-face or through live video-conference technology. Courses are designed specifically for working adults who want to complete a degree on a part-time basis while being able to balance career and family commitments. Great Valley MBA faculty teach the courses and typically alternate between physical campus locations where they teach from.

VLN Technology

Technology and instructional design are the foundation of any successful course offering through the VLN. For the online component of courses, Penn State's learning management system (LMS) is used to deliver online instruction. Through the use of integrated LMS tools and third-party software and applications, the goal is to create an engaging online experience as a complement to the synchronous class sessions.

A majority of the VLN technology is focused on the high-tech classrooms and its high-quality video-conferencing capabilities. Each VLN classroom is equipped with a networked system that can be manipulated through the control panel located at the instructor's podium. The control panel allows the instructor to project and broadcast content across participating site locations through connected computers, external devices, document camera, and video players.

In each VLN classroom, a camera located in the back of the classroom captures the teaching, even following the instructor's movements across the front of the classroom. A camera located in the front broadcasts a wide frame view of the students in the classroom, so connected sites see the instructor and students. A high-definition monitor in the back of the classroom allows the instructor teaching to see students from other participating locations, and one in the front allows the students to see peers from other sites, furthering learning connections.

To broadcast audio, the instructor uses a wireless microphone, and each VLN room is also equipped with directional microphones. Students can zoom the directional camera and focus the directional microphone to allow the student speaking to be heard and seen clearly at all locations.

A benefit to the audio- and video-classroom technology is that it allows the face-to-face class sessions to be recorded. Twenty-four hours after a class, a recording of classroom interactions across sites with broadcast content is accessible. Students sign a waiver at the beginning to allow the recording of class to take place.

VLN Course-Design Process

Considering the level of technology involved with managing multiple student sites, courses needed comprehensive redesign. For example, the cohort-based VLN MBA at Great Valley and Berks employs a clear sequence of courses, all of which needed redesign to take advantage of the hybrid, multisite pedagogy. Great Valley faculty provided course author and subject matter expert responsibilities, as they worked with instructional designers throughout the entire process.

The first step to course development included educating faculty about the VLN model along with strategies for teaching and learning in a hybrid environment. Faculty were enrolled in a four-part faculty training course that allowed faculty to experience the VLN from both the instructor and student perspective. Thus, faculty reflected on the needs of the students while learning the VLN technology.

The training also served as an opportunity to rethink teaching and apply hybrid course design principles. They learned new strategies for teaching via live video, which included classroom management across sites, incorporating class discussions and presentations, and adapting content to be broadcast clearly through the classroom technology. As a culmination of the training course, faculty deliver a sample lesson in the VLN classroom and collect feedback from peers and instructional designers.

Faculty then prepare their course for delivery in the VLN. Being a hybrid course, the focus of this phase is creating a cohesive and engaging learning environment by blending online instruction with the synchronous class sessions. Courses typically took a flipped approach for engaging face-to-face class sessions and appropriate online content and activities.

The lead instructional designer created a development plan and set benchmarks or milestones along the way to ensure courses are completed and open according to the set schedule. All class details, no matter how small or large, need to be properly planned for to ensure a successful student experience. For example, if an instructor traditionally would have students sign up for groups or research topics in class, this cannot be easily facilitated across multiple sites connected through video. Planners can set up an online approach to ensure students from all connected sites are involved in the process equally.

This development process allows the faculty to focus on the course content and teaching while leveraging the expertise of the instructional designer to adapt the instruction to a VLN format and handle the development of any online content or integration of instructional technology. By having these clear roles and responsibilities and working collaboratively through the course-development process, a quality hybrid course can be offered to students while empowering faculty to teach in a new environment.

Benefits and Challenges of the VLN

One of the benefits of the VLN is that, by expanding the reach for programs, PSU can reach student enrollment goals. In addition to growing tuition revenues, the VLN leverages existing PSU resources to control costs.

But the partnerships also come with challenges to sort out before implementation. Communication between partnering campuses is crucial in maintaining consistent messages to students regarding program expectations. Tasks such as student registration, revenue sharing, and technical support need to be carefully thought out with clear processes established.

Technology is certainly a consideration during the implementation of the VLN. PSU could leverage existing classroom technology to minimize the investment necessary to fully equip VLN classrooms. With a complex network of connected classrooms, technical support plays a crucial role. Support early in the development process is needed for faculty training. In addition, technical support is on call during class sessions to ensure there are not any connection issues and to help troubleshoot and assist as necessary. With any technology, issues are bound to arise, so it is important to be proactive and prepared with alternative plans if necessary.

Student Impact

From a student perspective, the VLN model offers its own set of benefits and challenges. One of the greatest benefits is the ability to retain the quality and experience of reputable traditional and face-to-face programming for student learning. Students interact and connect with Great Valley faculty and have the same learning experience, only from an alternate campus location. With the Great Valley and Berks campuses being an estimated sixty minutes apart, teaching faculty often alternate the main location that they teach from to further strengthen the connection with students.

With the hybrid format, VLN offerings appeal to New Majority students who seek a balance of flexibility and structure in their learning. Working adults who need to manage work, personal, and academic responsibilities experience the best of both worlds when it comes to online and traditional face-to-face learning. The ability to record the face-to-face class sessions allows for additional student flexibility. With possible inclement weather, last-minute conflicts, or work-related travel, students can still experience class via the recordings. Furthermore, the recordings allow students to revisit key concepts or review instruction from class if necessary.

The hybrid format is a great way for working adults to transition back into being a student while starting to build an acumen for distance learning. Regardless of the student, the VLN hybrid model is unique given that students are learning via live video. There can be a learning curve to the technology and overall structure of the course. To avoid frustration, program expectations should be clearly communicated along with a recommended orientation for new students to the VLN format. During the first classroom session, faculty should reserve time to allow students to practice and get used to communicating via the VLN room technology.

Overall, unique delivery models, such as the VLN, give institutions additional opportunities to leverage existing resources and infrastructure to expand program offerings to new student populations. Through proper planning, allocation of resources, and comprehensive instructional design, institutions have the potential to create creative solutions that offer New Majority students quality learning opportunities with technology and distance education.

RESTRUCTURING ROLES AND STRUCTURES: HIGH-IMPACT PRACTICES ADAPTED FOR ADULT LEARNERS

At Cabrini, a small, traditional liberal arts college, the challenge was to create an adult-learning baccalaureate program. Cabrini sought to solve two primary design challenges: serve New Majority learners in ways the other programs were not and employ portability to reach these niche clients across the metropolitan area. The approach needed to be sufficiently innovative to capture the imagination of faculty who could see themselves working differently both in the classroom and in the course preparation stages.

Designers started with the notion that the traditional classroom could be an inelegant design: the faculty member's human effort is out of proportion to the effort of the students, who were both capable of and eager to take more responsibility for their learning if it meant that the environment would be more customized to their goals and more respectful of their lives and experiences.

A new model for delivering adult learning, called the adult-education access pedagogy, uses a variation of a blended-learning environment. The main difference was that faculty members inhabited the online environment, and learning mentors (who are skilled in facilitation, but not content experts or faculty members) inhabited the face-to-face space. Another design feature was that during the face-to-face sessions, the courses would be essentially linked, but in the online environment the courses were separate. In this way, students could complete two courses, attending class only once a week.

What was particularly innovative is that the faculty members would collaborate on the actions that would happen in the mentor-supported face-to-face sessions and ensure that the instruction showed how the learning in the courses could be integrated and mutually supporting.

Access pedagogy is a product of design thinking, specifically aligning human effort (who is the best person to accomplish the essential work) with technology (how can technology support human effort and accomplish work that humans can't or shouldn't be doing) with sustainability (how can the effort-technology relationship be scaled while retaining high-quality outcomes).

An example illustrates the format. A cohort of students was simultaneously enrolled in a course on leadership and supervisory skills (a business class) and a course on food waste and insecurity (a general-education requirement). Students engaged with each faculty member in the online environment during the week, absorbing and applying content as one might expect in an online course. At once-weekly evening sessions, the students met together in the classroom, with guidance by a learning mentor, to solve problems using content from both courses.

During one week's online lesson, students in the business class learned about strategies for engaging and training employees and learned about the problem of food waste in the grocery industry in the social justice class. During the face-to-face session, students were challenged to create a training presentation for employees of a grocery store, educating them about the opportunity to divert food that would have been discarded to hungry mouths. The learning mentor guided the students, asking questions and encouraging students to work together to create a solution to a challenging problem.

The learning mentor supported the students in taking ownership for their active learning and making space for high-quality faculty interactions, which focused on how experts use the subject, what they find beautiful and useful in this way of seeing the world, and how students can be engaged as potential future colleagues who also celebrate and refine this disciplinary knowledge. Because they are not trained in the content areas, learning mentors serve as a kind of "near-peer" to show that the learning is possible and practical and to demonstrate successful learning strategies. The model shows how to apply the learning across boundaries. In this way, adult learners develop strategies to be successful in subsequent accelerated and online courses and also learn how to connect to communities of learners in and out of the classroom.

They also serve as a kind of "concierge" for adult learners, who are only on campus for a limited time and may not be aware of resources or opportunities. Learning mentors are ambassadors for the campus and can help students to make important connections with other members of the campus community.

Through expanding the notion of the human effort available in an adult-learning–centered classroom, energies to devote to high-impact practices were freed up. Learning mentors take on the effort of ensuring that students could use the technology, answering questions about campus services, registration deadlines, and even parking, and managing classroom-management tasks (taking role, returning papers, giving tests, etc.). By completing these low-impact tasks, learning mentors allow the faculty to increase efforts in formative feedback, aligning learning across the program of study, and making important college-to-career connections.

This model also creates a "flatter" authoritative structure rather than a traditional "sage-on-the-stage" model of instruction. Adult learners have likely had experiences in formal and informal leadership; grounding their academic pursuits (i.e., accounting, criminology, English, management, psychology, etc.) in leadership theories is an approach to offering the graduates opportunities to move into positions of authority in their designated career areas. This innovation strengthens adult learners' satisfaction with the learning environment, and it also allows for economies of scale that support the economics of the adult-learning program.

As with the VLN, the approach also required redesigning the use of technology and classroom space. In a blended course, online learning takes the place of a number of the traditional class meetings. At their best, a hybrid class assigns content and processes to the most appropriate learning environment for the students. For example, in a course where students are new to a field of study and need to take in content information, the online part of the course is likely a good fit for that kind of learning. In this way, students can consume the content at the rate they need and in forms that set the stage for persistent learning.

The face-to-face sessions are opportunities to apply that content under the guiding eye of the faculty member who can reinforce good thinking and pose probing questions. A hybrid class can benefit adult learners by reducing the time required to be on campus and by allowing for adults to spend more concentrated time with reading and writing assignments. However, adults, especially those who have been out of formal education for long periods, may need more directed guidance in using the technology and in prioritizing tasks. Fully online courses provide adult learners with freedom in how to allot their time to complete requirements.

Many adult learners have made the choice to return to college not only to get a degree but also to form new connections with other adults. They often have an idealized image of college in mind, and learning in a classroom with professors to guide them is part of that vision. Moreover, many adults have low levels of knowledge of college, and they need to connect to the college to build help-seeking behaviors and an understanding of the resources available. Finally, fully face-to-face classes can feed the need for connection and guidance from professors. But they can also pose barriers for adult learners, including pressures for verbal responses when the adult learners have a need for more processing time, self-doubt about being able to compete with other students, and physical discomfort with traditional desks and chairs in the classroom environment.

The adult-education access pedagogy draws on the best of both environments and then adds two additional values: connection and self-direction. Typically, in a face-to-face class, an instructor meets with the students for approximately three hours a week, and faculty tell students to study for two hours for every hour in the classroom, or a total of nine hours a week. The access pedagogy model divides the nine-hour-a-week commitment into three spaces: (a) the online learning environment, (b) self-directed learning, and (c) face-to-face time.

In the online environment, and in occasional virtual visits to the face-to-face environment (i.e., synchronous online activities), the faculty member

- Clarifies expectations and learning goals.
- Directs students to resources to meet those expectations and accomplish those goals.
- Explains how experts use resources and checks students' understanding as they use them.
- Relates the learning to the students' goals and to professional expectations beyond the classroom.
- Provides sustained formative and summative feedback to support the learners' growth.
- Conducts assessments and grading activities.

In the self-directed environment, and in occasional one-on-one communications with faculty members, the mentor, and other classmates, the learner engages with the resources: online materials, the textbook, out-of-class activities, and so on. In a traditional classroom, this would be what we would tell the learner to do when "studying"—reading the book, asking questions, doing research, writing papers, studying for tests, forming a study group, and so on.

The face-to-face environment, roughly three hours a week shared between the two intentionally linked courses, focuses on what would be called "homework" in a traditional class. In a traditional class, students get homework (low-risk, low-point-value tasks) to check emerging understanding. Homework provides just-in-time feedback and correction and gives students opportunities to apply the learning. The active learning experiences in the face-to-face sessions achieve these same goals: complete low-risk, low-point-value tasks that provide opportunities for the faculty member, in collaboration with the learning mentor, to check learners' emerging understanding. It's homework, but it's in "our house"—the classroom—and it's guided and facilitated by the learning mentor, not the faculty member.

Continuing the previous example, partway through the semester, students were told that they would be asked to create their own plans for a food-recovery program targeted at grocery and restaurant facilities that generate less than fifty pounds of surplus food. Their plans would be presented to a local nonprofit that was working on solutions to the food-waste problem. Initially one student was vocally resistant, arguing that it wasn't appropriate for students to be making presentations to outside groups. Instead of "squashing" the conversation, the learning mentor encouraged conversation about the question. Eventually other students spoke up and argued that this was an exciting opportunity to put what they were learning to use. The class took ownership of the project and ended up delivering highly professional plans at the end of term.

This approach is not only grounded in transformational learning theory, which is discussed in chapter 7; it is also a model of good andragogical practice. Students who have been working or tending to family all day or all week can come to a classroom where they do more than sit and listen or sit and talk. They move around the room, find and use resources, and connect their learning to their lives and goals. They can use their maturity and leadership in the classroom and experience working in highly effective teams to reflect on social and work issues.

Not only does this access pedagogy impact the way students learn, it also changes the "faculty math," allowing individual faculty to be spread over a larger number of students, potentially in different locations. The learning mentors replace some faculty effort, allowing faculty members to devote more of their time on high-quality engagement with a slightly larger number of students.

The access pedagogy asks faculty to restructure their courses and become familiar with their new roles and relationships. In addition to creating paired assignments, it may seem odd to faculty for a learning mentor, who is not an expert in the class material, to be interacting with students. But faculty adjust, and find new ways to benefit from the mentor's presence. For example, the faculty member teaching the leadership class was initially surprised by how students approached a discussion prompt at the beginning of the semester. The faculty member discussed this with the mentor, who then probed the class and helped uncover some unexpressed reservations about the assignment (that the students did not volunteer to the faculty in the online mode).

BETTER LEARNING, BETTER FINANCES

In both the PSU and Cabrini examples, existing university resources were restructured to create an academic product designed to meet the needs of New Majority learners. For PSU, the target learner was a returning adult student who was not accustomed to a fully online course. The VLN approach provided a relatively traditional in-class experience. The format allowed students attending local branch campuses (that are typically close to home and work) to conveniently access top university professors, who would not normally be available at the local branch campuses. The learning experience was student centered and tailored to the needs of New Majority learners.

For Cabrini, the adult-education access pedagogy allowed learners to access information and learn in ways that were tailored to adult students. In-person class meetings create opportunities for students to build learning communities, whereas the learning mentor represents a "more capable peer" who can model good practices. The integrated assignments enable students to work together to apply and understand content in an active learning environment. Having multiple face-to-face mentoring sections allows the pedagogy to be presented at multiple locations within a region, providing the convenience that New Majority learners need.

In both cases, programs use existing resources. Existing faculty teach their normal subjects but in slightly different ways. Campus technology is more heavily leveraged. For the VLN, the real-time connections between classroom locations becomes critical. But the classroom and technological infrastructure existed; it just needed to be used and supported in different ways. Faculty needed additional support from instructional-design staff to identify new ways to engage students in this virtual environment. And technical support needed to be available at the time and place where the courses were offered.

For the access pedagogy, faculty needed to learn to teach and engage with students differently. The addition of a learning mentor changed the teacher–student dynamic but opened opportunities for improving the classroom dynamic. Existing technology was used for the online components, but the support needs were not unique. The learning mentor role was new, but they were easily recruited from adults who served as adjunct faculty or tutors at local institutions. The learning mentor also acted as a "guide" to campus support services and so filled a broader role as well.

In a market with many fully online players, campuses need to explore ways of offering a differentiated product that meets student needs and leverages existing institutional strengths and resources. Both VLN and access pedagogy required people within the institutions to dare to do things differently but demonstrate that a repurposing and restructuring of existing resources can create new learning products with the potential to fill emerging market needs. As we will see in the next chapter, universities can also look externally to find new and potentially more efficient ways of meeting student needs.

KEY POINTS

- Change requires doing things differently, so roles and structures can be altered to create new learning environments that leverage existing resources to deliver new educational products.
- Technology can be used to transform the idea of a classroom space. PSU's VLN connects students on branch campuses with a main-campus faculty member to create an expanded classroom. This format uses technology to connect senior faculty with more students, allowing for increased access and lower overall costs.
- An adult-education access pedagogy creates a new teaching role, that of learning mentor, to model good practice, demonstrate that success is achievable, and act as intermediary between teachers and

learners. By adapting high-impact practices to the needs of adult learners, a transformed environment serves the needs of New Majority learners.

NOTES

1. https://stats.psu.edu
2. http://news.psu.edu/story/156562/2011/07/28/york-adult-learners-earn-first-certificates-through-vln
3. http://greatvalley.psu.edu/this-is-penn-state
4. http://berks.psu.edu/penn-state-berks-glance

SIX

Administrative Redesign: Human-Centered Design Applications for Sustaining Change

Marguerite Weber and Beverly Schneller

In chapters 3 and 4, contributors explored both the cost-of-learning and student-centered redesign. This chapter builds on those concepts and introduces the idea of applying cost-of-learning and course-redesign principles to reimagining academic administration. Briefly, redesign means openness to rethinking everything to determine what is the best configuration of human effort, technology, and financial resources, where *best* is defined as a system that reliably produces needed results without error and without waste of time, energy, and goodwill.

The rise of New Majority learners in higher education has impacted student expectations for their experiences in and out of the classroom, the cost and revenue bases for sustaining the institution, policies to enforce accountability for outcomes, technologies, and cultural attitudes toward consuming and supporting higher education. At their peril, administrators adapt a business-as-usual approach to leading their institutions through these high-impact challenges. That is because New Majority students bring different strengths, experiences, and needs and because, of course, they are a new plurality among students.

Academic administrators have three primary functions: (1) attend to the quality of the student experience in and out of the classroom to ensure that learners succeed; (2) manage resources (friends and funds) to ensure the institution is sustainable; and (3) keep up with emerging issues in technology, demography, workforce development, policies, and economics to scan for threats and opportunities.

Leaders connect the campus community to powerful learning experiences that inspire all to conceive efficiencies by reforming how work gets done on the campus. They engage campus thought leaders in assessing emerging technologies and data sciences to refine the quality of decisions and eliminate waste. Finally, they envision the kinds of investments that bring returns in knowledge, innovation, and the value proposition of the institution's mission and core values.

Change propositions require collective, coordinated, and coherent strategies to overcome internal inertia. Some spark that change by rethinking what students, faculty, and staff do in the learning environments. They may be guided by learning from other industries or bringing in external partners to solve for what their community members can't or shouldn't do alone. Some deploy disruptive technology to make good use of new sources of data to inform practices or new tools to scale what works. Still others will break through the boundaries between institutions and find success in a sharing economy. Some will draw on all three approaches.

ACADEMIC TRANSFORMATION AND ADMINISTRATIVE REDESIGN

Course redesign, the most prominent initiative to come out of academic transformation efforts, has yielded tremendous gains in the classroom (see also chapter 5).[1] The present chapter argues for higher-education institutions to engage in *administrative redesign*, using human-centered (HC) design principles, to realize gains in access, equity, success, and sustainability. A brief review of how academic transformation principles apply to course redesign is a good place to start to prepare to understand how they apply at the larger institutional level.

Instructional-redesign practitioners reimagine learning processes to keep costs fixed while promoting higher gains in measured learning or expanding access while keeping costs flat or nearly flat. Simply put, the goal is to either increase the number of seats available or the amount of demonstrated learning with no additional financial investment and no loss to learning effectiveness or to maintain the number of seats and the learning effectiveness while reducing the cost. The strongest redesign projects accomplish both increased measures of learning effectiveness and reduce the cost per seat.

The first step in HC design involves describing human effort within the system through accounting for all the roles (i.e., teacher, student, staff, paraprofessional aides, etc.) contributing to the productivity of the system. The first level of analysis looks at what people in those roles can do (without excessive error), will do (given a specific level of reward), and should do (within a specific ethical construct). Designers then look to reimagine the roles or to expand the roles to include additional or different support and then identify what, even after the reimagination, humans still can't, won't, or shouldn't do.

The next step involves integrating technology that can augment what humans can't do (by helping to eliminate errors and by expanding capabilities or reducing time on task), what they won't do (by making the work easier or more attractive or by eliminating the human effort all together), or what they shouldn't do (by making the work anonymized or by eliminating conflicts of interest, for example). The final step centers on assessing the cost and productivity of the new system and aligning levels of resources to support it.

The end game of HC design is finding the most efficient design that can produce needed outcomes, consuming only the resources available to sustain the function. In other words, HC design is intended to eliminate waste, and once the system is consistent in producing value on sustainable resources, HC design principles demand that the tinkering stop until conditions materially change (i.e., a new competitive environment, new technologies, threats to resources, etc.). In this way, HC design runs counter to continuous-process improvement or the endless closing of assessment loops.

Administrative transformation can be similarly realized through the principles of HC design. Some examples here have redesigned human effort, some employed technology in innovative ways, and others altered the financial models to achieve institutional goals.

REDESIGNING HUMAN EFFORT THROUGH INNOVATIVE PARTNERSHIPS

One way to engage in the "human" part of HC design is to engage in innovative partnerships that have increased learning, access, equity, and productivity. The first two examples are from historically black colleges and universities (HBCUs): one shows an alliance between higher education and a government agency, and the other explores a partnership with a for-profit organization that builds social capital and academic success skills for New Majority students in transition. Finally, there is an example that addresses a partnership centered on addressing faculty and staff initiative fatigue at a rural community college.

Founded in 1900, Coppin State University (CSU), in Baltimore, Maryland, evolved from a two-year teacher's college into an urban, residential, historically black university (HBU). CSU is a New Majority–serving institution. President Maria Thompson describes the CSU "human" climate:

> We will always have the residential experience because we have students who want the "letterman jacket" experience. But most students are working, many raising families. We need to ensure that education

can be a seamless part of their lives. And we are realizing that we also
have a multigenerational workforce coming to work . . . from different
vantage points.[2]

Previously, at Tennessee State University (TSU), Thompson showed
uncanny ability to envision and energize innovative partnerships. As the
vice president for research and sponsored programs at TSU, Thompson
formed a partnership with the state's flagship institution, the University
of Tennessee (UT), and the Oak Ridge National Laboratory (ORNL).
Thompson describes the work:

> We started with the shared goal of producing more STEM graduates
> from underrepresented student populations. We recognized the mag-
> nitude of our scope in contrast with the resources of the flagship cam-
> pus, and decided that our niche strength was that we had a student
> population that was in demand by industry partners.[3]

This partnership centered on getting more underrepresented students
into sciences, and what was innovative was the commitment to use the
partnership for mutual borrowing. "Faculty and resources from each contributor had to be unique, and none of us would duplicate what the other
already had." In this case, TSU had the underrepresented students; UT
had facilities and faculty for applied and theoretical sciences; and ORNL
had the latest and most-expensive technologies (and a need to prepare
future scientists to fill positions at all levels).

To start, the partners needed to reimagine assumptions of leadership.
"In a partnership, there is always the presumption that there is a leader."
Instead, as Thompson explains, "we all have to recognize each other's
strengths. We're in a partnership with equal actors in it."

This approach was a success; according to Thompson,

> At some point we even started to forget who worked for whom be-
> cause the students were at the center of everything we did. We saw
> ourselves as part of a puzzle that would make these students at the
> center, whether they became Ph.D. scientists, workers in science labs,
> or even undergraduate interns. We wanted to assume the role of the
> next step in their lives and development as professionals.

As an example of using design thinking to refine the partnership arrange-
ment, TSU needed students to have access to an expensive high-powered
microscope. Instead of buying it, the partnership arranged for remote
access to the technology at ORNL. The solution ensured underrepresented students had access to the industry-standard technology that neither
TSU nor UT could have bought. It also used technology to augment human effort. The faculty could explain authentic work environments, but
the partnership provided one. Students worked side by side with ORNL
technicians to use their learning to solve real problems.

The partnership also reimagined technology and the business case. Referring to the remote-access solution, Thompson notes, "Technology not only made these kinds of collaborations possible. It made them necessary. Because this is how we work."

The impact on the business case extends beyond avoiding redundant equipment expenses. UT avoided expenses for recruiting, retaining, and developing responsive services for underrepresented students. ORNL avoided expenses for building a pipeline for diverse students with authentic training and experience. TSU avoided expenses associated with setting up additional internships and student faculty research opportunities.

Fast-forward to CSU, where, in 2015, Thompson became CSU's seventh president. One of the first large-scale partnerships that Thompson engaged in was an alliance with Bridge.Edu, a company founded by Wes Moore (of *The Other Wes Moore* fame) to strengthen the transition experience of urban first-generation college students.

For Moore, the impetus to create Bridge.Edu was an equity issue: wealthy students who wanted time to explore interests before committing to a college could afford a "gap" year filled with travel, experiential learning, and networking opportunities. Their connections not only provided knowledge of college but also gave them the kinds of cultural capital that supported them in risk-taking explorations. [4]

With a higher-education landscape of high attrition and high student debt, Moore reasoned that the neediest students could not have access to the knowledge, skills, and support that were needed to succeed. Bridge.Edu incorporates mentors, coaches, and "battle buddies" to support students through academic-skills development and career-exploration opportunities; in addition, the work is supported by a proprietary YesU app that gives students guidance, advice, and practical approaches to affording the colleges where they are a good fit and likely to thrive.

Finally, Bridge.Edu, a for-profit organization, supports first-generation college students in developing knowledge of college and skills for productive persistence. Bridge.Edu students' successes contribute to CSU's measures of institutional effectiveness (retention, developmental placements, loan default rates, etc.), but they also become meaningful role models for other students because they have developed habits of leadership and mutual support.

President Thompson calls the Bridge.Edu partnership "one of our most important partnerships," in part because the students have intentional exposure to the work of people who operate outside of higher education and because Bridge.Edu provides learning experiences that CSU could not replicate internally.

However, the partnership was not without its controversy. Thompson explains, "There was push back on campus for partnering with a for-profit. They would say, 'What is this?' Why are we paying someone else

to teach our students?' I'd point out that we have lots of for-profit partners on campus—Aramark, Barnes & Noble, Subway, etc." To Thompson, it's a partnership that helps CSU do good and do well by supporting
at-risk students with relevant and enriched services and experiences and
by shifting costs to an external expense.

"More people have to understand that higher education is a business.
And this business is impacted by the external operating environment,"
Thompson says. "We not only have to be able to compete with other
higher-education institutions, but with other sectors of the economy that
can create the same [experience]."

Thompson indicates that she learned much about the partnership im-
perative from Nancy Zimpher, chancellor of the State University of New
York System: "She focused on the 'systemness' concept. Start with serving students better and then collectively serve more students by expanding whom you can reach. 'Systemness' means executing seamless rather
than discrete initiatives." At that level, leaders can think differently about
how to assemble units. Thompson summarizes:

> What's important is to start with the goal: serving students better and
> then collectively serving more students. Then move to structure. When
> you start with how to serve current students better, you start to evalu-
> ate where there are areas that other campuses do well and who are
> partners that want to do better. Then we team up. We look to the
> partners to work together to provide resources and to identify what
> none of us has and find out how we can get that. Resources are always
> described as limited, but we need to talk about how they can be a
> multiplier.

One area where institutions need a ready multiplier of human capacities
is the challenge of using increasingly large data sets on student demographics and success patterns to shape initiatives to improve institutional
effectiveness. The last example in this section explores a college–consultant partnership that uses HC design to expand decision-
maker capacities, technology to cocreate projects, and work sharing to
control costs.

A challenge for community colleges is creating time in faculty and
staff opinion leaders' heavy workloads to allow for insightful reflections
on data, best practices, student success literature, and strategies to pursue
teaching as a craft. The very faculty whose insights and experiences are
necessary for executing initiatives to sustain and transform the institution
are those whose time and energies are heavily invested in daily student
involvement. And too, these committed educators are also those who
might not care to engage in what might seem to be *administrivia*—the data
dives, the policy analyses, the outcomes assessment, and the budgeting.

Add to this picture some important historical shifts. Changes in faculty demographics—"boomer" senior faculty retirements, shortages in

midcareer faculty because of historical budget constraints, increased reliance on adjunct faculty—mean that the "usual subjects" for faculty leaders are often tapped to take on multiple change and college service projects.

Meanwhile, although many academic administrators come from faculty, their career trajectory and professional development efforts were likely built on aggregating knowledge of the whole institution of higher education, its best practices and inner workings and its "systemness." Therefore, their teaching and learning efforts have shifted to building internal talent, influencing external stakeholders, and meeting resources.

The urgency to serve ever more students with ever more academic, financial, employment, and support needs and to keep up with competition for ever more diverse students has resulted in institutions taking on effectiveness-improving initiatives all at once. The "new normal" is coordinating a wide range of grants and improvement initiatives, some of which will be abandoned when special funding runs out. College leaders need support in strategies to embed promising practices into the college culture and to support the organization's learning from them to make subsequent initiatives increasingly efficient.

Northeastern Oklahoma (NEO) A&M is a public, residential two-year college in rural northeastern Oklahoma that offers transfer-friendly associate-degree programs as well as occupational programs for graduates to enter the workforce immediately. NEO is a New Majority–serving institution, serving first-generation, racially diverse students, most of whom work while attending school. It is a Native American–serving, nontribal college.

Faced with pressure from statewide efforts to improve retention and completion and to reduce or eliminate remediation, even for students who do not test as college ready in reading, writing, and mathematics, NEO decided to engage in a partnership with Higher Learning Design (HLD), a consulting group that contributes data analysis and change-management support (initiative design, prioritization, capacity building, implementation, and assessment).[5]

Although using a consultant to supplement administrative capacities is not innovative, the approach that NEO took provides a good example of how to realize academic transformation through reimagining human effort. Project Director Rachel Lloyd explains the benefit:

> For a small, rural, poor college, this type of arrangement is logical and strategic for many reasons. For one, if we were to hire someone full-time, we couldn't afford the talent [HLD has] to offer and the individual wouldn't be able to produce the quality of deliverables . . . in the same amount of time.[6]

NEO took a "gig economy" approach to using resources to acquire just the skill set needed and for just the appropriate amount of time while creating highly individualized institutional learning experiences developed to promote sustainable transformation.

The first step of the project involved using HLD as a means to multiply institutional research resources. Institutional researchers were well poised to gather data on the characteristics of successful and less successful learners at the course- and degree-completion levels. However, because their role at NEO had focused primarily on accountability reporting, they had gaps in knowledge and experience with best practices in retention, closing achievement gaps, and completion initiatives.

HLD analyzed the data and then embarked on a series of "listening sessions" with faculty and staff to determine ways that the data could inform NEO's choices in what projects to start immediately, which to assign later priorities, and which to put on hold while building institutional capacities for change.

The initial decision was to have faculty work on course-redesign projects in developmental writing while staff in first-year services (i.e., orientation, advising, first-year seminar, etc.) undertook a remaking of transition experiences. NEO faculty and staff, together with HLD, engaged in day-long visioning workshops to understand and adapt principles of academic transformation to the two-pronged approach. The work will continue in phases to include student support services redesign, first-year programs restructuring, and innovations in the cocurriculum.

The partnership is an example of HC design, not only because it used data to assess what the people in the environment (faculty, administrators, staff, students, paraprofessionals, and the consultant) could, would, and should do, but the work has also made good use of communications, information, and course-management technologies to bridge distance, time zones, and differing levels of insights and capacities to get the work done efficiently.

TECHNOLOGY TO SCALE ADMINISTRATIVE EFFORT

HC design incorporates strategic use of technology to augment human effort, to make efforts sustainable, or both. The examples in this section include a partnership between a university and regional employer to create an entirely new institution. A second example shows a model for using technology to mine massive data sets to make actionable predictions for student success, thus allowing institutions to transform themselves to anticipate emerging needs.

Howard West, launched in March 2017, is a collaboration between Google and Howard University (an HBCU located in Washington, DC) that brings talented young black computer science students to Silicon Valley to work side by side with Google engineers.[7] The program goal is to increase diversity in the workforce and provide a platform for leadership development from among underrepresented populations in the industry. It is comparable to Georgia Tech's MS in computer science program offered in partnership with online educational provider Udacity and AT&T, composed entirely of nine MOOCs.[8]

In 2005, FedEx launched the FedEx Institute of Technology (FIT), a partnership with the University of Memphis (UM). FIT promotes faculty–student research and learning around global commerce and its intersection with the development of new technologies.[9] Published current research, including work on smart cities, drones, and big data, shows how the FIT work benefits UM scholars and FedEx practitioners.[10] As part of their technology transfer efforts, the FIT licenses innovation to industries. They have produced twenty-five US patented applications, fifteen licenses for stakeholder uses, and more than 147 invention disclosures.

The FIT's HC design is best seen in their sponsored events, which range from "Critical Skills Workshops" to "Memphis Technology Foundation User Groups" where participants discuss uses and advances in "Gaming Development; Python; R; Data Science/Machine Learning/Artificial Intelligence; Ruby; WebWorkers; and WordPress." FedEx with the UM is looking to frame the future of data analytics, engage in broad-based technology development, and advance the culture of global business through development of students as researchers with future-focused habits of mind.

In 2014, Georgia State University (GSU) decided to act on persistence, retention, and graduation through partnering with the Educational Advisory Board (EAB) Student Success Collaborative. EAB supports academic improvement in the HC modalities, whether the topic is the validity of early-alert systems, professional development of academic leaders, or as in this case, how to improve retention and graduation rates. The GSU project set goals of a 60 percent graduation rate by 2021, which would save the university millions of operating dollars, and they are well on their way to achieving that goal.

EAB's Student Success Management System is grounded in data analytics, and through a college-centered analysis, the EAB team and faculty use the metrics to discover the strong and weak links in the curriculum and in student dispositions and learning abilities. The intent of the resulting Student Success Collaborative (SSC) system is to build student support networks on the campus that will enable students to "make smarter choices" about their learning experiences.

The support will increase student satisfaction, which in turn, will improve graduation rates mainly by reducing swirl (or student's changing majors or institutions as they search for the right fit). There are more than 450 SSC members, who receive customized consulting and the opportunity to gather at the CONNECTED conference to share best practices in the use of early-alert, learning-support, and divergent-degree pathways.[11]

Many other campuses have engaged with EAB to improve advising, adjust prerequisites and course sequences, set priorities for course redesign, deploy faculty development, and other academic transformations. EAB offers campuses a way to outsource the design thinking for their learning-support infrastructures. It also creates a space for academic leaders, student affairs, learning-support staff, and others charged with improving institutional effectiveness and student-learning outcomes to share ideas and explore alternative solutions to campus-specific issues such as those of GSU with retention and persistence to graduation.

SYSTEMNESS AND THE BUSINESS CASE FOR HIGHER EDUCATION

So far, the discussions of Bridge.Edu, Higher Learning Design, and EAB have shown relatively common fee-for-services models to multiply administrative resources within the context of helping campuses achieve broader desired goals. This section explores the "business case" of higher education with a focus on the larger-scale collaborations in the form of multicampus consortia.

These consortia arrangements evoke the qualities of the contemporary sharing economy, wherein collaborators seek to reduce the need for redundant processes and resources by agreeing to reimagine notions of ownership and separateness. They provide a means to realize efficiencies in human capital, facilities, and monetary resources, essentially determining that cooperation bests competition in today's higher-education climate.

In 2012, sixteen liberal arts colleges from the Associated Colleges of the South, formed the New Paradigm Initiative, with goals to share costs of technology, extend the pedagogies of established distance-learning courses into face-to-face classes through synchronous learning, and build collaborations intended to raise perceptions about the quality of online learning. They started with lower enrolling curricula, such as languages, where there is a need to cut costs because of lack of revenue but at the same time, continue to give students access to in-demand languages, such as Arabic[12]—and the notion of multicampus consortia has expanded.

The Pennsylvania Consortium for the Liberal Arts (PCLA) received a three-year $800,000 grant from the Mellon Foundation in 2014 to form a partnership across ten smaller liberal arts colleges to reduce instructional costs, promote collaboration across the schools, and improve measured student-learning outcomes.[13] The ten participants were Franklin & Marshall, Swarthmore, Dickinson, Gettysburg, Juniata, Bryn Mawr, Haverford, Muhlenberg, Ursinus, and Washington & Jefferson colleges.

Modeled along the same lines as the New York Six and Massachusetts' Five College Consortium, the PCLA allowed faculty to share expertise and resources, and offered a network of like-minded opportunities for collaboration and teamwork in learning design. One example of their collaborative projects is the Language Commons Technology Learning Space at Muhlenberg College,[14] which, like the New Paradigm Initiative, uses technology to provide capacities to expand language learning.

Within the small liberal arts schools, and predating the PCLA, is the Tri-College Consortium of Bryn Mawr, Swarthmore, and Haverford, all located within driving distance of one another on what is known as the Main Line outside of Philadelphia, Pennsylvania.

Students in the Tri-College Consortium can share libraries, enroll in classes on one another's campuses, and expand their course offerings by allowing students to study in fields not offered on an individual campus. The resource sharing addresses instructional costs and has the potential to reduce swirl in two ways: by offering students a way to study other subjects without transferring and increasing their sense of community by allowing access to participate in the student experience on each campus.

By 2014, a group called Liberal Arts Consortium for Learning Online, made up of Amherst, Bryn Mawr, Carleton, Pomona, Haverford, Swarthmore, Vassar, and Washington & Lee colleges formed with this mission: "Through collaboration, we are exploring new models of teaching and learning in the service of residential liberal arts education."[15] They indicate they are reaching sixteen thousand students combined and use slightly more than two thousand faculty in their collaborative efforts.

This consortium focuses on the ability to "share, collaborate, experiment, and connect" students, faculty members, and resources to deliver innovative and unique educational experiences that enhance four specific learning areas: quantitative literacy, active reading, language instruction, and effective teaching and learning.

Minnesota provides another example of an intra-institutional consortium with partnerships among Concordia College, Minnesota State University–Moorhead, North Dakota State University, North Dakota State College of Science, and Minnesota State Community and Technical College. The program is an articulation agreement allowing "course exchange as a means of supplementing the preparation and completion of a degreed program or the transfer to a partner institution."[16]

This cooperative, formed in 1962, has partnered with the YWCA and water-systems development groups, earned grants, and supported humanities programming across the campuses. In 2007, they had enabled more than thirty-two thousand students to participate in course exchanges, which they estimate represents about 5 percent of the student bodies on each campus.

Because of the rapid growth of massive open online courses (MOOCs) since 2010, there have been numerous endeavors to replicate learning experiences traditionally located on college campuses in the online world. Providers such as Coursera introduced their Signature learning program to demonstrate the quality of their course participants' learning in ways that would produce a transcript of their online courses as equivalent to terrestrial transfer courses. Other providers offer badges, certificates, and online curriculum sequenced to replicate a traditional degree.

Udemy and EdX are developing degrees, especially in business, and are facing accreditation challenges as they seek US university partners, and Facebook announced late in spring 2017 its intention to offer college-level courses.

In 2015, Colgate University and Hamilton, Wellesley, and Davidson colleges signed an agreement with EdX and became the Liberal Arts Learning Consortium Online. The four colleges were early adopters of MOOCs, and the consortium allows for course exchanges as well as a means, through EdX as the data-management platform, to provide a way to warehouse course materials and information on teaching and learning for participating faculty.[17]

A PROVOCATION

The common interests across these collaborations center on improving student learning, cost sharing, and resource maximization. Although it is arguable that articulation agreements have been serving this purpose for decades, the focus and the need for HC design will only increase as the New Majority learner populations do, and it is incumbent on higher education to find ways to acknowledge the learning styles, needs, and interests of their student populations and to find ways to make earning a college degree affordable across the socioeconomic spectrum.

Accreditation agencies will need to become more flexible or change their focuses entirely to finances and assurance of learning, thus narrowing their purview to the things that an external review can really address: whether the curriculum is benefitting the students and if the programs are properly funded.

It is hard to define "quality" and "student success" to begin with because each individual student on each campus in their own geography is a unique individual. If institutions were evaluated on how well they designed learning environments and funded them, it would be much easier for collaborations to develop and survive. Merely reducing duplicative programs does not increase access or improve learning; however, reducing duplicative programs while building capacity in consortial partners will serve to strengthen the quality of the academic programming and allow for focused hiring and targeted uses of resources.

Instead of pushing against collaborations such as Coursera, the liberal arts colleges and universities would do well to closely examine the relationships between their business model and the Oxford tutorials and start considering how they could leverage the qualities of each campus's unique instructional voice to attract and retain students who not only need, but also want to have their say in what they are taught and why.

WORKING FROM WITHIN: SUSTAINING THE CHANGE

Consortia and cross-functional collaborations are hard to sustain, and the assurance of learning that is expected with them can be problematic. Creating networks for delivering more options to students, to get and hold their interest in higher education, remains important for the future of liberal learning.

No one has the potential to be more adversely affected by change, yet positively influenced toward change than the smaller liberal arts colleges that dot the US educational landscape. Sadly, in the last five years, some smaller colleges have had to close or significantly downsize, largely because of declining enrollments, tuition discounting that does not keep pace with operational costs, and for some, reductions in state revenue.

As the example of President Maria Thompson shows, facing the establishment mind-set extant in many corners of the academy is an act of courage and a risk to one's leadership. However, academic leaders, together with faculty, alums, and broader community stakeholders, need to listen to one another and work collaboratively to support one another. A healthy competition for students will continue to drive positive change for the academy and will have the potential to drive up the capital (both human and financial) to make higher education sustainable for the future.

KEY POINTS

- Change propositions require collective, coordinated, and coherent strategies to overcome internal inertia, so employing the principles of academic transformation to administrative redesign is a means to sustain New Majority institutions.
- In administrative redesign, New Majority institutions go beyond the usual suspects to find partners that can serve as resource multipliers; in these innovative partnerships, collaborators take a *systemness* approach to determining right-sized effort and sharing leadership.
- New technologies have yielded new resources for data collecting, mining, and sharing; academic redesign takes advantage of emerging technologies to refine systems and improve their productivity and effectiveness.

- The notion of *systemness* can also impact the business case for higher education; a sharing economy approach among institutions can scale resources and improve the financial health of all partners.

NOTES

1. National Center for Academic Transformation, http://www.thencat.org.
2. Maria Thompson, personal interview with M. Weber, May 31, 2017.
3. Thompson, personal interview.
4. Wes Moore, personal communication with M. Weber, March 2013.
5. http://www.higherlearningdesign.com
6. R. Lloyd, personal communication with M. Weber, December 6, 2016.
7. M. Basely, "Are Today's Students Prepared to Enter the Tech Industry?" *Center for American Progress*, July 23, 2017, https://www.americanprogress.org/issues/race/news/2017/06/23/434758/todays-students-prepared-enter-tech-industry.
8. "Learn Computer Sciences from Georgia Tech," http://www.udacity.com.
9. M. Corbet, "FedEx Commits $3 Million to Technology Institute," *BizJournal*, March 30, 2015.
10. http://www.memphis.edu
11. http://www.eab.com
12. J. Selingo, "A Liberal-Arts Consortium Experiments with Course Sharing," *Chronicle of Higher Education*, April 4, 2012.
13. B. Miller, "10 Liberal Arts Colleges in Pennsylvania Form Consortium," http://www.pennlive.com/midstate/index.ssf/2014/07/10_liberal_arts_colleges_in_pe.html.
14. http://www.pcla.org
15. http://www.lacol.net
16. http://www.tri-college.org
17. C. Straumsheim, "A Liberal Arts Take on Tech," *Inside Higher Ed*, May 13, 2015, https://www.insidehighered.com/news/2015/05/13/four-liberal-arts-colleges-early-mooc-scene-form-online-education-consortium.

SEVEN

Planning and Executing: Navigating Change at New Majority–Serving Institutions

Marguerite Weber and Eric Malm

When adult or first-generation learners were only a small subset of the student population, many schools, built for traditional first-time, full-time students, made small internal reallocations to run parallel programs (evening, weekend, and online) for nontraditional learners. If the mission of the institution embraced both access and equity, these sideline programs might create distinctive learning opportunities that would still be economically sound if staffing costs were low. So, they employed part-time scholar-practitioners who could connect to students with rich life experiences but had tenuous connections to the institutions themselves.

But the demographics have shifted. The plurality of students at many institutions now can be identified as New Majority. Their needs for immediate workforce skills, durable abilities, and equitable access to high-touch, transformative experiences have become a central focus for institutions facing diminishing pools of the "usual suspects" for recruitment. And more and more of the usual suspects are also "shopping" for practical, adaptable degrees and experiences with demonstrable value for their education investment.

There are other cataclysms too. New technologies transformed teaching, learning, communicating, marketing, and internal processes. Competition for students' attention is fierce. For-profit and nonprofit schools offer traditional credentials, but there are also alternative credentials, including competency-based badges and certificates that are becoming increasingly respected for workforce readiness. Emerging analysis tools make available ever more real-time, nuanced, and actionable information, demanding that leaders develop data-science capacities for the decision making that in prior years had been driven by anecdote, experience, and instinct.

And the workforce in higher education is changing as well, with burgeoning midlevel leaders to manage marketing, communication, institutional research, and assessment functions and a growing reliance on contract and adjunct workers and faculty. The rapidity and scope of these changes should make it obvious that "business as usual" in higher education is a sure path to obsolescence.

One reviewer of *Academic Transformation: A Design Approach for the New Majority* asked, "Is anyone focusing on redesigning institutions to serve students better? It's becoming a key aspect of all this work—you can describe the students, provide best practices, etc., but unless you address structure and process in your institution, it won't happen."[1] Previous chapters here addressed large-scale applications of redesign, but this chapter centers on strategic planning for more whole-cloth transformations for sustained change.

The logic is this: if institutions are truly facing a shift in student demographics so that those with adult-learning challenges represent a majority of students, then for an institution to be effective, shouldn't everything be put back on the table? That is, given the new normal of New Majority learners, institution-wide strategic priorities should be subject to open discussion, and there should be both a willingness and a plan for the campus mind-set to shift. Consequently, new ways of planning and executing strategic initiatives are equally necessary.

THE SELF ON THE SHELF: STRATEGIC PLANS THAT ARE NEITHER STRATEGIC NOR PLANS

Many have decried the failures of strategic planning. Beach and Lindahl summarize more than twenty years of critiques of strategic planning in higher education.[2] In citing a 2012 study they note, "60% of organizations do not link strategic planning to budgeting, 75% do not link employee incentives to strategies, 86% of business owners and managers spend less than one hour per month discussing strategy, and 95% of a typical workforce do not understand their organization's strategy." But planning goes on, like an unexamined ritual.

Even when colleagues collaborate within a responsive governance structure to work together on specific, measurable, appropriate, relevant, and timely (SMART) goals, and where strategies and initiatives are cleanly aligned with goals and with available resources, even then, strategic plans remain problematic. The complicating issue is creating the plan in a "bottom-up" manner with the business-as-usual assumption that things will continue as they have and that the student-learning product that the institution was created to deliver will remain mostly unchanged. The strategies, then, are largely tinkering at the margins.

Students, technologies, workforce needs, and contemporary culture are changing so rapidly that by year two, any five-year plan is likely a dusty afterthought. At New Majority learner–serving institutions—and let's face the fact that this distinction is pervasive enough to stop noting here—strategic plans are, at best, outdated and irrelevant when they are completed and approved by the campus. At their worst, they can be constraining.

A typical approach to improving responsiveness is the ubiquitous strengths, weaknesses, opportunities, threats (SWOT) analysis as a precursor to developing a full strategic plan. A SWOT analysis, also called SWOC (replacing "threats" with the kinder and gentler "challenges"), has the benefit of checking goals and plans against internal and external realities. Taking the time to center future planning against predictors of future impacts is time well spent. However, it is an insufficient precaution because it takes place at a single point in time and lacks the power to be more continuously dynamic.

Another patch for inherent flaws in strategic planning processes is monitoring key performance indicators (KPIs). Process owners make ongoing measures of student enrollment behaviors and academic achievement and count participation and outreach relative to initiatives centered in emerging best practices or trend data for peers. They periodically make reports of their individual measures and communicate progress. An example of how one might knit KPIs to strategies and then the weaknesses of relying on this approach at New Majority–serving institutions can be explored as follows.

Let's say an institution decided a primary strategic goal would be to narrow the achievement gap in graduation rates between majority and an underrepresented population in the sciences by 10 percent in five years. The strategies and KPIs might include these:

1. Incorporate open educational resources (OER) for the first-year seminar to include more diverse readings about science discoveries. KPIs might include the number of faculty who complete the integration of OER and between-group data on the pass rates for first-year seminar, the incidence of declaring science as a major, success in gateway courses for science majors, and so on.
2. Train academic advisors in the sciences on issues involving cultural sensitivity. KPIs would monitor advisor engagement, self-reported use of their training in modifying advising protocols, student satisfaction with advising (from the NSSE), and enrollments in science.

3. Provide book scholarships for students with a 3.0 GPA and low socioeconomic status by their third semester of continuous study. KPIs might be faculty reports of student preparation for the major, grade distributions, and attrition (again with between-group data).

This is a worthy plan with credible KPIs, so flaws here are not attributable to the intrepid planners. Rather, it is the nature of the KPI as a tool of measurement that can undermine the security of a strategic plan.

First, actionable data is too long in coming. In this example, for full-time, continuously enrolled students, the span between the faculty implementation of OER to even the grades in upper-division courses will be at minimum three, but more likely, five years. For New Majority learners, those who may be overrepresented in the underrepresented group, the time is likely much longer because of their being more part-time and more likely to start and stop because of access and affordability issues.

The second flaw in reliance on KPIs is that when the initiatives are as sweeping as those in the example, it is nearly impossible to determine which lever did the trick in closing a gap. How would a decision maker know what to continue to invest in or what to pull? What was the single best initiative, or best combination of actions, to yield the needed return on investment? Because many organizations expand outreach to New Majority learners because they face plummeting enrollments from traditional learners, there is rarely a resource to waste. Funding initiatives without a laser focus on results tests resolve to make sweeping changes.

Yet, a planning model, called *strategic* or by another name, is needed for leaders to monitor how well they are keeping promises made to their students, and as the competition for students and their attention heats up, the more reliable and agile that information is, the better poised the organization will be to respond.

THE BALANCED SCORECARD AS AN ALTERNATIVE TOOL FOR STRATEGIC PLANNING

The rise of the assessment movement in higher education in the 1990s and subsequent increased calls for accountability for student persistence and completion outcomes set the stage for drawing comparisons between higher education and business sectors. Consequently, the tools and measurement practices gaining popularity in the business world were increasingly employed by higher-education institutions, often as a patch or an add-on for a quick demonstration of institutional effectiveness.[3]

One such tool is the Balanced Scorecard (BSC), introduced by Robert S. Kaplan in 1992 (figure 7.1). The BSC is an improvement because it provides a means of inquiry into institutional health from four perspectives: financial, internal business processes, innovation and learning, and customer needs and expectations. Another advantage is that the institution's vision and mission are at the center of planning and measurement approaches.

This diagram centers the four monitoring systems on the organization's vision and strategy. That is, to think in terms of Sinek's Golden Circle,[4] the organization starts with "why" (the vision), and the "why" drives the "how" (the strategy) it will use in striving to achieve the vision. The shared core values foundational to the vision and strategy inform what work is accomplished from each of the perspectives. For example, with a shared value of inspiring transformational learning, each perspective would be driven to contribute its efforts to that goal.

- Knowledge and innovation generators, typically faculty, instructional designers, and institutional researchers, among others, would center work on what approaches to learning best guide students to acquire relevant content, to practice and assess essential processes that use that content, and then to achieve the kind of growth and confidence that enables deep inquiry into the premises of knowledge domains.
- Marketing, admissions, orientation, advising, and student-affairs planners would spend energy to educate prospective and new students on the value of the distinctive learning opportunities, and

Figure 7.1. The Balanced Scorecard (BSC)

student-development practices would then likely center on resilience, self-management, and leadership development.

- Financial priorities would create and support conditions for transformation, including capital investments in different kinds of classroom spaces that promote collaboration and meaningful inquiry-based learning. There would be funds for visiting scholars and speakers and for the high-impact practices that inspire deep learning.
- Internal business processes would likely be marked by a flat authority structure, with smart use of technology and data deployed to supplement the work of decision makers, thus freeing as many human resources as possible to be student facing.

Working around the circle, business/process owners serve internal customers. For example, "customer satisfaction" (the needs and expectations of students, employers, accreditors, board members, etc.) informs and directs both the "knowledge-and-innovation" workers and the "financial-performance" workers. Managers who oversee financial performance direct and limit resources available for internal "business processes and efficiency." Those customer needs, financial performance, and the efficiency of business processes all impact the product—academic credentials created by the organization.

Academics who were uplifted by the extended discussion of the transformational learning example and then queasy at the subsequent reductive business case will immediately grasp a problem with transposing a tool that was built for business onto the aspirations of higher education. As Stewart and Carpenter-Hubin explain, "Translating the balanced scorecard to the complex world of academia is a challenge."[5] They continue, "Skepticism exists on campuses regarding the notion that a university's performance can be measured quantitatively."

Another likely element of resistance to business measures being applied to the work of higher education is the real danger of a learning organization falling into initiative fatigue. Engaged participants in change management across the institution would be involved in research, inquiries, pilot activities, and assessment efforts focused on best serving needs at the circles on either side. Even though they often engage the same reliable "workhorses" on campus, those efforts are unlikely to be coordinated or sequenced. Possibly because it was born from an assumption of a businesslike hierarchy, the BSC is inscrutable in giving direction for priorities.

Finally, another flaw in applying a commercial tool like the BSC directly to higher education is the issue of "ownership" of the strategic objectives, strategy map, performance measures and objectives, and strategic initiatives weighted at the bottom of figure 7.1. Where are the connections that would reflect typical campus governance structures? The business BSC assumes a stratum of leadership at the thirty thousand-foot level to be the ultimate consumer of the data and performance measures generated, and to have the final say.

This chapter has not come to bury strategic planning in higher education, but to praise it. When college community members collectively analyze evidence and data of student learning and success, they will be more prepared to make decisions on transforming institutional structure, resource-management practices, policies, and work processes. What's needed is a refashioned strategic and balanced tool to support administrative redesign and change management.

BORROW FROM THE BEST: THE BALANCED VALUES CANVAS FOR ACADEMIC TRANSFORMATION

Change activities are only as good as the data and assumptions on which they are planned. Macroeconomists sometimes talk about "adaptive expectations" compared with "rational expectations" modeling. In an adaptive-expectations world, consumers and businesses assume that the world will go on as it always has. It is backward looking, and when results from the current period don't match hopes, a minor adjustment is made, and "We'll get 'em next time." Thus, they adapt to shocks slowly.

In a rational-expectations world, organizations collect data on current and expected future conditions and make more forward-looking decisions. They can adapt rapidly and engage in survivable risks that move the organization forward.

An asset of the business BSC is that it is designed to facilitate this responsive forward-looking risk management. However, in much of higher education, there is a deep cultural bias against reducing the energies of public intellectuals to counting beans or customer service. Therefore, the language and top-down assumptions of the business BSC can have the limitations of confounding communication and constraining buy-in.

One way to take advantage of what works in the BSC is to more clearly translate the business terms in the BSC into concepts that are more easily recognized and valued by higher education. Another is to align some strategic planning KPIs as consensus-building tools that are useful to campus governance conventions.

However, although the BSC defines connections between perspectives for facilitating how stakeholders communicate expectations, an effective adaptation for higher education needs a way to recognize natural tensions between the perspectives. If left hidden, these tensions can contribute to a wasteful environment of blaming, gamesmanship, and power plays. Reckoning those tendencies into a new BSC, the Balanced Values

Chapter 7

Canvas (see figure 7.2) creates opportunities for productive academic transformation in higher education.[6]

What follows is an analysis of differences between the business BSC and the Balanced Values Canvas by exploring the quadrant spaces formed by the intersections through mission and values.

Vision, Strategy to Mission, and Core Values

The subtle shift here denotes that a clearly articulated mission is the primary means through which higher-education institutions differentiate themselves from peers. In the business BSC, the vision may change with leadership, but at a college or university, the mission endures beyond any change in presidency. The mission is what allows a president to tell senior staff that their job is to sustain the institution for five years while the president wakes up every morning thinking twenty years out.

In the business BSC, the term *strategy* is how the company will respond to market, political, economic, and technical forces. Generally, it means how they will compete to carve out a sustainable market share.

In the Balanced Values Canvas, core values define the organizational culture. Shared values guide who joins the community (students, faculty, and staff) and inspire them to form bonds; they shape the look and use of materials and facilities; and they serve a kind of self-editing function for

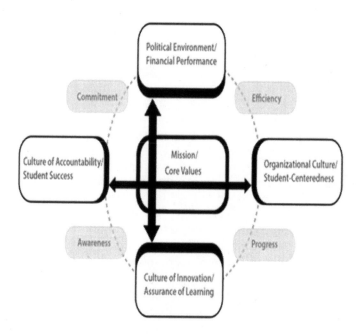

Figure 7.2. Balanced Values Canvas

winnowing initiatives. Planners from the perspectives around the circle start with determining if a proposed change is consonant with the core values before they proceed to advocate for resourcing that idea.

Customer and Stakeholder "Satisfaction" to a Culture of Accountability and Student Success

In the business BSC, the customers are generally conceived of as external forces. Like accrediting boards, local employers, feeder schools, government, funders, and others who evaluate an institution's value proposition and delivery of brand promise, our student prospects are also external. But then those same students enter our organization and impact our effectiveness, productivity, and reputation.

The Balanced Values Canvas captures this duality. The culture of accountability refers to the tools that external constituents use to determine whether they will form an initial commitment to the school and the strength of that commitment. Student success refers to the degree to which students are aware of the value of the learning and aware of the expectations they will need to meet to achieve their goals. Measures of commitment create opportunities for strategic initiatives that move the institution to more fully realize its mission and core values.

Measures of external stakeholders' commitment can include employer satisfaction of graduates, meeting accreditation standards, and even admissions yield for various populations. Financially, the commitment could include yield on grant proposals, donor contributions, government funding and voter support for that funding, and the growth of productive partnerships. With those measures, strategic planners can then frame experiments that are guided by the organization's mission and core values and by best practices at peer and aspirational institutions to close the gaps between the current and goal measures.

Measures of matriculated students' commitment can be defined by counts of behaviors associated with initial and subsequent commitment.[7] Depending on the institution, behaviors related to initial commitment could include the fit of precollege characteristics with those of retained students, attendance at admissions open houses and orientation, and even first-semester attendance, self-reported study and engagement time, and course-management system tracking of on-time assignment submission. A story is in order.

Dr. Maria Thompson, president of Coppin State University (CSU), instituted the Data Democratization Project.[8] She noticed a campus narrative about the students' needs that ran counter to the measures of commitment and awareness she had access to. Therefore, she transformed her "Executive Dashboard" into a "Campus Dashboard" to provide the entire campus with access to the same key metrics that she and her staff wrestled with every day.

For example, faculty could now evaluate program requirements using data on the impact of credit-hour requirements. They learned that in some academic programs, a large number of their students left CSU without a completed degree because they ran out of financial aid; faculty engaged in program reviews and refinements to address this issue.

CSU created opportunities for professional development in understanding the data and aligning efforts to the story the data told. Thompson explains that she fancies herself "story-teller-in-chief" and leads the institution with stories and data, "but it's up to the employees within the institution to write much of the text." With accurate measures of commitment and awareness, and in an atmosphere that encourages dialogue about change, she and her campus can construct a new story about a bright future for the university.

Consider how the Data Democratization Project well mirrors ways that business is using more real-time data to make strategic decisions. For example, Best Buy created an employee social networking site called "Blue Shirt Nation" with the idea that if executives could glean information from the 100,000 employees who are talking to customers on the floor each day, they'd be able to make better decisions. Similarly, fashion retailer Zara uses both real-time analytics (both of what's selling and what's not) and a system for collecting customer feedback from store managers to continually change their product production decisions.

Note, too, how President Thompson incorporated effective models for New Majority learners' engagement in the learning environment created for CSU *employees*. They had a practical, job-related need for learning, but there were access and emotional barriers to their engagement. Employees balancing multiple responsibilities had an urgent need to develop new technology and numeracy skills. Thompson supported extensive professional development in multiple formats, including individualized tutoring, group coaching, face-to-face instruction, and self-paced online learning.

Financial/Stewardship and "Performance" to Political Environment and Financial Performance

In the business BSC, this block means "How do we look to our shareholders?" For those in higher education, this category really captures concerns about maintaining or achieving long-term financial viability while maintaining stability with mission and core values. In other words, "How much mission can we continue to buy?"

The change between the business BSC and the Balanced Values Canvas is nuanced but important. Here's an illustration.

According to a National Association of College and University Business Officers (NACUBO) survey on tuition discounting, about 68 percent of chief business officers cited the *price sensitivity of students* as being the leading cause for declining enrollments.[9] Others cite the endless escalation of the arms race in student accommodations—the ubiquitous rock wall of our imagination. Thus, the business BSC would likely see financial threats as beyond the control of the institution. This view likely would result in prioritizing marketing and branding activities that would impact how the institution looks to "shareholders."

However, the Balanced Values Canvas would help the organization to do two things. First, there would likely be a push to collaborate with knowledge and innovation creators on initiatives that impact the value proposition of the credential. The value proposition is how students become informed consumers to weigh the gain against the price. Soliday and Mann explain, "Schools with a strong value proposition are not necessarily inexpensive, but their cost is perceived as an excellent value for the outcomes provided by the experience."[10] Reasoning in this manner might lead to structural changes including competency-based learning, revenue-sharing agreements, expanding advisory councils to ensure that programs align with workforce values, and tuition-discounting alliances. In other words, "How do we increase our value to those who need our mission?"

Second, they would work to influence internal business processes to ensure that no amount of student time, energy, or goodwill would be lost to unnecessary barriers to progress. They would carefully scrutinize processes that primarily promote employee convenience to determine if any of them unduly burden students.

Internal Business Processes and "Efficiency" to Organizational Culture and Student-Centeredness

Like the financial-performance attribute in the business BSC, in the Balanced Values Canvas "efficiency" is a continually shared concept. A difference, however, is that in the business view, efficiency denotes meeting customer and regulatory expectations with the absolute minimum of investment. In the Balanced Values Canvas, efficiency means administrative/academic redesign of the type explained in chapter 6.

For example, an urban community college engaged in administrative redesign in student affairs to transfer energies from supervision to student engagement. It started with analyzing the functions of each office in the division, which included all admissions, financial aid, records and registration, veterans' affairs, TRIO and Upward Bound programs, freshman advising, athletics, student governance, wellness, Title IX/judicial affairs, disabilities services, and student-life activities.

The analysis started with the functions aligned with goals for the student experience. Those activities were then assessed for their scope (the degree to which they engaged all groups of students, including evening, part-time, online, and satellite campuses). And then assessed for the degree to which they accomplished stated goals.

Finally, the team executed a values-centered redesign plan. Any vacant supervisory position was evaluated to distribute those responsibilities (with salary increases) to other experienced employees. Where possible, technology solutions made those supervisory responsibilities more efficient and less prone to error, and new positions were created to serve students directly, thus flattening the administrative structure and improving capacities to respond to students with no additional costs.

In his *Harvard Business Review* article "Why Do Employees Resist Change?," Paul Strebel stresses the idea of personal compact. A personal compact represents the implicit agreement between an employee and employer and is related to the brand promise between a brand and its consumers. According to Strebel,[11] a personal compact has three dimensions: formal ("What do I have to do?"), psychological ("How will these changes impact how I do my job?"), and social ("How might this change impact why I choose to work at this institution?"). It's worthwhile to consider any change within the lens of the personal compact.

The changes described are no exception. This community college achieved the academic transformation goal of increasing capacities for student engagement at a fixed cost not because of the determination to find savings, but instead, the success depended on redesign for student impact. As at CSU, expanding opportunities to use and understand data and challenging passed-around failure narratives with measures of student progress, created savings and camaraderie.

Organizational Capacity and "Knowledge and Innovation" to Culture of Innovation and Assurance of Learning

This account has come around the circle of the Balanced Values Canvas without even a nod to two distinct differences between figures 7.1 and 7.2: the "tension" arrows linking positions and the values-words in the spaces between positions.

The business BSC depicts service relationships that flow through each perspective. The Balanced Values Canvas continues to see the interconnectedness of the positions but acknowledges that there is a productive tension between sets of perspectives. The primary tension exists between the political environment and financial performance and the culture of innovation and assurance of learning.

Tired tropes about faculty members going to the "dark side" to become officious "bean counters" or about obdurate faculty incapable of coming out of the ivory tower to appreciate the school's business fundamentals are common markers of this tension. Instead, what's needed is a practice of using one perspective to refine the aspirations of the other. Consider this: it was largely the political pressure to eliminate remediation, condemning it as causing taxpayers to have to pay twice for teaching, that sparked the creative energies of the redesign movement.[12]

Thinking about using tensions between value perspectives is like using game theory in the classroom.[13] Without constraining rules, a game isn't possible because there would be no barriers to help players devise or improve strategies to overcome them. And there are no measures of winning. Leaders responsive to political and economic forces and responsible for the institution's finances need colleagues dedicated to innovation and assurance of learning to burnish their strategies for aligning resources with the mission and core values, and vice versa.

In describing innovations in learning approaches in chapter 5, the authors declare: "[These approaches] required people within the institutions to dare to do things differently, but demonstrate that a repurposing and restructuring of existing resources can create new learning products with the potential to fill emerging market needs."

The case is stronger when business and market terms interlace with concepts familiar to innovation and assurance of learning. Indeed, the access pedagogy is an example of this approach. One of the more innovative aspects of the pedagogy is that it is "portable and supportable." Learning mentors facilitate the face-to-face sessions and faculty the online learning, so hybrid courses are offered at multiple sites.

This design had the business advantage of filling more seats and a lower cost than it would take had there been faculty at each site; it also solidified creative partnerships between the university and community colleges, resulting in savings in marketing and recruitment. But there were also gains in learning. The model takes after the Vygotskian notion of employing a more capable other to bridge the gap in authority between the teacher and the student, resulting in students' adapting autonomous learning habits.

The Balanced Values Canvas shows a similar productive tension between student success and student-centeredness, an unusual juxtaposition, because frequently these terms are conflated. The intention of the opposition is to highlight the danger of being blind to competing goals.

Once again, consider remediation. At institutions serving large numbers of students who test as "not college ready" in reading, writing, and numeracy, a whole "cottage industry" of support has developed: the remedial courses themselves, tutors, special advisors, TRIO programs, and so on. Colleagues thus engaged rely on the institution to recruit students who aren't yet college ready, and if the students need to take the courses more than once, then that further fills seats in remedial sections.

On the other side are calls for increasing student success, measured in large part by on-time credential attainment. These colleagues strive to recruit the best students possible, those who have the precollege characteristics associated with completion. They need completers to highlight in their brochures and in accountability reports.

Without engaged problem solving between colleagues from these two perspectives, the internal organizational culture of student-centered services would naturally be characterized by enabling learners' sense of helplessness and need. The students' needs for protection would likely become the unifying call from this side. The student-success side would likely use "hero stories" to celebrate improbable (and at times unrelatable) stories of brilliant exceptions. Both approaches result in undermining student resilience and work ethic, both necessary components of overall institutional health and effectiveness.

Instead, consider an example of the strategic priorities of Northeastern Oklahoma (NEO) A&M, the two-year rural school introduced in chapter 6. They coordinate student-services support, enrollment management, administration, and faculty to center their problem solving on increasing resilience and undoing students' (and employees') learned helplessness behaviors. They refined onboarding materials to focus on personal accountability and work ethic and rigorously scrubbed out the narratives of the "hero" and "those poor students" from their interactions. That culture work set the stage for major revisions in advising, orientation, and remediation processes.

Explanatory Habits

The last feature of the Balanced Values Canvas is attention to the language of negotiation among perspectives. In education theory, the term *explanatory habits* means identifying if a student has a belief that both good and bad things that happen are caused by luck, happenstance, and others exerting power (external explanations or locus of control) or by personal effort, skill, and autonomy (internal explanations/locus of control).

In the Balanced Values Canvas, explanatory habits denote the latter. With conscious sharing of how work in one position is aligned with work in another position, these explanatory habits foster functional leadership[14] across units because they create spaces for consciously using the language and values of the other to communicate ideas.

"Commitment" is the shared value that connects the political and economic perspective to the external environment (accountability and student success).

To prospective students (and to the enrollment-management staff who work to secure them), commitment could refer to the institution's brand promise, and for a New Majority learner, that promise is likely to center on the increased financial rewards that will result from students' investing their tuition dollars. Those from the political and financial perspective will value return on investment (ROI), but may also see commitment as a rational decision to spend resources on efforts that impact yield from the enrollment-management funnel.

For example, at NEO, designers of advising, peer-mentoring, and faculty-development materials use the concept of ROI during orientation activities to articulate expectations for students' return on their investment of time, energy, and goodwill. Being explicit with commitment and the ROI on the strength of commitment is particularly effective with New Majority learners who are eager to have a clear sense of the effort expected when they are told to study. Used to having actions and investments of talents more explicitly communicated in the workplace, these learners appreciate a workmanlike approach to explaining their work.

The explanatory habit of efficiency links the political and financial perspective to the organizational culture and student-centeredness perspective. Consciously weighing the impact of effort on results is a habit that not only governs expenditures of money, time, and energy, but it also creates a climate of expectations for personal accountability, mutual support, and devising conservation plans that achieve good results with less effort.

What's important is that those from the organizational culture and student-centeredness in the Balanced Values Canvas approach have much to contribute to a discussion of smart investments and when it's foolhardy to demand doing more with less. For this partnership to be a strength during institutional transformation, these two positions need to be equal partners engaging in effectively designed solutions to resource scarcities.

"Progress" connects organizational culture and student-centeredness with innovation and assurance of learning because both of these perspectives align their work habits within a culture of adding value at each subsequent touch point.

Academic programs, for example, build on foundational capacities in lower-division courses, and students progress to near-peer relationships with faculty through the students' upper-division and perhaps eventually graduate studies. And too, with internal business processes, work moves through systems of creation and reaction through solution and approval. Linking internal work processes to knowledge and innovation creation can result in creative human-centered design solutions that help to transform the institution.

Student-affairs units also mirror this developmental approach to the student life cycle. Students at the beginning of the enrollment-management funnel may have only the vaguest impressions of the school. But then students move from recruitment, to admission, to matriculation, to early engagement and support services intended to strengthen their commitment to completion. At each stage, student-affairs experiences intend to build on students' capacities centered on belonging, security, and hope. These attributes prepare students for the next stage of development where they will develop skills in self-regulation, goal setting, and leadership.

As students near credential completion, student affairs solidifies college and career connections and workforce readiness. As they leave, students are reminded to be engaged alumni, ambassadors, and role models for the students coming up from behind them.

Finally, "awareness" is a shared value between innovation and assurance of learning and accountability and student success in the Balanced Values Canvas. To thrive, each of these positions needs the other position to be aware of the value of their effort and the relationship between effort and outcomes.

New Majority learners, for example, need the faculty to be aware of their work—the realities of their work responsibilities as well as the value of their work to their learning endeavors. Those faculty, too, need students to be aware of what constitutes academic work—what does rigorous intellectual engagement look like and why is it important? For example, if the student thinks that the quality of the product is all that matters, then how will they come to be aware of the consequences of academic dishonesty? The business of academic work needs to be laid bare for students who may be unaware of the values faculty hold dear.

Using the Balanced Values Canvas

The notion of making use of productive tensions and shared explanatory habits between and among positions sets the stage for the real work of planning academic transformation. The mode of thinking that underpins this approach is called abduction.[15] The central premise of abduction, as distinct from either deduction or induction, is that "new ideas can only be validated by the unfolding of future events."

As with the rational-expectations model, with abduction, "we must turn away from our standard definitions of proof—and from the false certainty of the past—and instead stare into a mystery to ask what could be." Designers and their collaborators use the past (i.e., data from prior cohorts) to form a hypothesis about the best solution to a problem that has not yet been solved. They go through a process to determine the strength of that plan.

- **Identify the paradox:** Why, despite best efforts, are students behaving in a certain way? Why is it difficult to recruit and retain diverse faculty? A paradox is confounding because past knowledge failed to determine a new course of action.
- **Devise an informed solution:** What practices can be borrowed from solutions in different industries or from different perspectives that be reimagined to resolve the paradox? As in chapter 6, what can FedEx teach the University of Memphis, and vice versa? The solution at this stage is neither true nor effective. Instead, it is a hypothesis in need of testing.

- **Take the solution to heuristic:** Through rigorous testing that yields actionable data, the proposition of the solution is refined into a "rule of thumb" — what is typically true when applying the refined solution to the paradox. At this stage, however, the solution is inefficient because it hasn't yet become the way things are done (it's a pilot).
- **Integrate the algorithm:** Moving the heuristic to algorithm, something that is sustainable and replicable, requires incorporating it into the processes, policies, and resource structure of the organization and doing away with the tired nonsolutions that created the paradox in the first place. The organization reduces waste by leaving the system in place as long as it continues to resolve the paradox.

PRODUCTIVE TENSIONS AND TRANSFORMING INSTITUTIONS

Integrating the language and values of higher education into a Balanced Values Canvas makes productive use of the tensions between perspectives. The tensions reveal gaps in the sufficiency of past knowledge and experience to inform the kinds of deep structural changes that will be needed for organizations that were originally built to serve traditional students to shift ideas, culture, premises, and resources to the needs of New Majority learners.

Those organizations that do engage in rethinking everything rather than only in serving students' new needs with sidelines and window dressing will be poised not only to thrive but also to support a renaissance of higher education in the future.

KEY POINTS

- Whole institutions can engage in redesign efforts to serve students better, and they should, considering cataclysmic changes in student demographics, technologies, and the competitive landscape.
- Traditional higher-education processes and practices, as well as planning tools adapted from the business sector, are insufficient to support transformation at the institutional scale.
- The new Balanced Values Canvas could serve as a framework for large-scale transformation work because it addressed our academic values and culture and the frequently conflicting efforts to respond to internal and external forces and stakeholders' needs.

NOTES

1. Marie Cini, personal correspondence with M. Weber, June 29, 2017.
2. R. H. Beach and R. A. Lindahl, "A Discussion of Strategic Planning, Change, Reform, and the Improvement of Education," *Educational Planning* 22, no. 2 (2015): 13.
3. A. C. Stewart and J. Carpenter-Hubin, "The Balanced Scorecard: Beyond Reporting and Rankings," *Planning for Higher Education*, Winter 2000–2001, 37–42.
4. https://www.ted.com/talks/simon_sinek_how_great_leaders_inspire_action.
5. Stewart and Carpenter-Hubin, "The Balanced Scorecard," 42.
6. http://www.higherlearningdesign.com.
7. J. M. Braxton, A. S. Hirschy, and S. A. McClendon, *Understanding and Reducing College Student Departure* (San Francisco: Jossey-Bass, 2004), 43.
8. Personal correspondence.
9. R. Seltzer, "Discounting Keeps Climbing," *Inside Higher Ed*, May 15, 2017, https://www.insidehighered.com/news/2017/05/15/private-colleges-and-universities-increase-tuition-discounting-again-2016-17.
10. J. Soliday and R. Mann, *Surviving to Thriving: A Planning Framework for Leaders of Private Colleges & Universities* (Grand Rapids, MI: Credo Press, 2013), 68.
11. P. Strebel, "Why Do Employees Resist Change?" *Harvard Business Review*, May–June 1996, 86–92.
12. C. Twigg, "Increasing Success in Developmental Math: Following the NCAT Playbook," 2008, http://www.thencat.org.
13. B. E. Shelton and J. Scoresby, *Aligning Game Activity with Educational Goals*, Utah State University, 2008, http://digitalcommons.usu.edu/cgi/viewcontent.cgi?article=1134&context=itls_facpub.
14. F. P. Morgeson, D. S. DeRue, and E. P. Karam, "Leadership in Teams: A Functional Approach to Understanding Leadership Structures and Processes," *Journal of Management* 36, no. 1 (2010): 5–39.
15. R. Martin, *The Design of Business* (Cambridge, MA: Harvard University Press, 2009), 25.

Appendix

Workbook Discussion Guide

Beverly Schneller

This appendix offers suggestions for seminars, workshops, applications, and further reading on the themes and topics of this volume. Each workshop is arranged with a theoretical framework, concept, or approach augmented with activities, outcomes, and ideas for further reading. These pages are meant as starting points and to offer guidance, not to prescribe or dictate.

The readings for each chapter are representative. There are many interest groups, educational-learning tool purveyors, and others whose work you may want to examine for the latest in conversations that are most relevant to your campus's needs. For example, the *Chronicle of Higher Education* 2017 report, "The Future of Enrollment: Where Colleges Will Find Their Next Students"; Sandvine Corporation's 2014 "Global Internet Phenomena Report"; Hart Research Associates's 2015 "Falling Short? College Learning and Career Success"; and Lumina's 2016 "A Stronger Nation: Postsecondary Learning Builds the Talent That Helps Us Rise" are just a few of the resources you can explore to continue the conversation on design thinking, sustainability, and the future of higher education.

CHAPTER 1: GETTING TO KNOW YOUR STUDENTS

The emphasis in chapter 1 is on getting to know who the New Majority learners are. Having established broad demographic traits, your campus may wish to start with a New Majority–focused SWOT analysis. Here are some starter questions:

- How many New Majority learners are on your campus? How much do key stakeholders on the campus know about the New Majority student populations?
- What are the main points of entry for New Majority learners to gain exposure to this campus and its offerings?
- Why do New Majority learners choose this campus?

- When New Majority learners enroll in academic programs, what are their goals at entry? Are their goals or aspirations met, or do they change during the course of their studies?
- Are we taking steps to incorporate their enthusiasm, interest, and drive for higher education when we create and review programs and courses?
- What might we do differently to reach our existing New Majority learners and attract others?
- Does it seem reasonable to build a team who is responsible for communicating information about the New Majority learners to assure a quality experience for all across the campus?

Network

The traditional partners in an academic SWOT analysis are in play here, too. But you may also want to invite your admission's office recruiters, your institutional research staff, marketing, and staff who have taken advantage of tuition benefits to earn their degrees while working to the table to explore ways you can demonstrate commitment to New Majority learners. Naturally, asking New Majority students to join the dialogue will have multiple benefits. Specifically, seek partners on campus who can help you shape what and how you communicate why New Majority learners will want to come to your campus, what you offer them, and how you have given their needs and interests a place in campus learning, support, and overall, campus experience design.

Action Plan

Launch teams to create storyboards narrating the New Majority students' experiences on your campus. Divide the boards up by gender, socioeconomic information, graduation rates, and concentrations in majors or colleges, to bring more than admissions information to the conversation. Your SWOT analysis will come from here as you deep-dive into what you do and why you do it and recognize one size may not always fit all students.

Use the storyboard narratives to create focus groups that will lead to highlighting New Majority students' exposure to, engagement with, and expectations for academic and cocurricular programming, learning support, academic policies, technology support and policies, and learning outcomes. Triangulate what you find with NSSE, CIRP, and other forms of student satisfaction surveys.

Partner faculty members in conversations with members of the financial aid office, admissions recruiters, the career center, and health/counseling services in campus workshops focused on reaching New Majority learners holistically. Come away with questions about how New Majority students see themselves as college success stories. This will include enriched awareness of what brings them to higher education, what they want as their experience, how to help them stay, and how to build on their choices to make their classroom and applied experiences linked and relevant to their reasons for enrolling at your campus.

Recognize your New Majority learners' champions and invite them to prepare a learning experience infrastructure that can be used as a tool to communicate with the whole campus about who is here and why we need to get to know them.

Develop a broader, strategic campus conversation, perhaps with the provost, registrar, adult degree completion leaders, or student affairs, on creative disruption and your campus's student body. What transformations in institutional best practices at any and all levels need to happen to engage everyone on campus in student success?

Outcomes

The main outcome for the explorations and actions suggested here is to uncover the assumptions about "students," what they need to thrive on campus, and what their behavioral characteristics are that cause the New Majority learners to leave or to persist to graduation. To continue with our lyrical metaphor, we really do want to "get to know all about them," because we need them to like us! Liking us means that New Majority students see our campus as a place where who they are, what they want, and what they need has been more than thought about. Rather, meeting the learning needs of all students is a priority which is present in programs, services, policies, and most importantly, pedagogy.

Campus Book Group

Bowen, Jose. *Teaching Naked: How Moving Technology Out of Your Classroom Will Improve Student Learning*. New York: Wiley, 2012.

Braxton, John, et al. *Rethinking College Student Retention*. San Francisco: Jossey-Bass, 2014.

Brint, Steven. *The Future of the City of Intellect: The Changing America University*. Stanford: Stanford University Press, 2002.

Cuba, Lee, et al. *Making Decisions in College: Practice for Life*. Cambridge, MA: Harvard University Press, 2016.

McNair, Tina Brown, et al. *Becoming a Student-Ready College: A New Culture of Leadership for Student Success*. San Francisco: Jossey-Bass, 2016.

CHAPTER 2: WHY CAN'T WE BE FRIENDS?

Beth Rubin's essay allows us to see the higher-learning design landscape. For our purposes, we are going to ask, "How do we incorporate the traditional models and modalities of the college and university curriculum into the interests of the New Majority in ways that fit their learning styles and needs?"

We encourage you to select from the questions that follow or create some like them. Depending on the time and size of the workshop, try starting in pairs, and then merge the pairs into small groups on the same themes to compare findings. For the reporting out, you may want to role-play scenarios or dialogues or provide the materials for a simple poster session-type larger group discussion with poster board, markers, and sticky notes.

In the end, you want to create a summary chart of four columns of information: (1) what are the issues that the exercise has defined, (2) what lies behind the issues, (3) what steps can you take to resolve or address the issue, and (4) who are the responsible parties for addressing the issues? For the final table summary, we are broadly indebted to the May 2017 TED Talk by Tim Ferriss, "Why You Should Define Your Fears Instead of Goals." He suggests what you worry about or are afraid of is a motivator in gaining a stoic's view of passion balanced with reason, allowing you to reach a neutral viewpoint within highly charged emotional and psychological situations.

Here are the prompts:

- As a member of this campus (based in role or duties), how do you believe the institution responds to change? Is there one unified approach to dealing with change or is the response dependent on some sense of magnitude or sweep of change?
- What is the one big thing you identify as needing to change on this campus?
- Describe what you know about your campus business model.
- What are your biggest and smallest challenges to sustaining your institution?
- To what extent can you describe your competition within your educational market?
- What draws students to your campus now? What patterns do you see? Are you able to distinguish different marketing and recruiting strategies based in understanding the types of students you are and want to be enrolling?
- Now, think about the nature of the curriculum on the campus. What have you done in the last five years to refresh the curriculum to keep pace with the learning styles, needs, and goals of the student body? Are you transparent in demonstrating awareness of and familiarity with the different types of students who are enrolled across your programs of study?
- If you completed the storyboard exercise on the New Majority learners' journey from the previous worksheet, what do you need

to tell the stakeholders about what you have gained from Beth Rubin?

Action Plan

There are multiple touch points and players who have some say in the business model, in the broad idea of competition for students, and in how the campus chooses what it will respond to, to spark change or transformation. A key in understanding your niche in a competitive world, no matter the product, is having a firm grasp of your brand and image. Your competitors can act like a prospective student, and many do just that by signing up for campus tours, accessing the website, and using IPEDs data and Guide Star to get the low down on who you say you are. What do your brand and image project?

Instead of eschewing change and competition, reach out to your alumni and ask them what they think about how flexible and transformation ready your institution was for them. Importantly, ask them what they would invest in (yes, as donors) and let them guide your development office in new or timely directions. Simply put, what would make Sereni a donor to her alma mater? If you give to your alma mater, why do that? What does that say about your concern for the competition and what you value? In a transient economy, what will encourage them to make your campus a site for their giving?

Outcome

We want you to take a hard look at who you are working for, what you are working toward, what you are communicating, and how the business models you have in place are helping or hurting your ability to pivot. We encourage you to look closely at the why, to borrow from Simon Sinek (http://www.startwithwhy.com) and use that as a way to inform decision making and learning design, so you can strategize how to make the best of the competitive environment in which we all find ourselves in higher education.

Campus Book Group

Dweck, Carol. *Mindset: The New Psychology of Success*. New York: Ballantine, 2006.
Yohn, Denise Lee. *What Great Brands Do: The Seven Brand-Building Principles That Separate the Best from the Rest*. San Francisco: Jossey-Bass, 2014.

CHAPTER 3: UNDER THE BIG TOP

Eric Malm, in "Defining Your University's Product," advances the prior discussion of brand and image from an economic standpoint, allowing you to think about the entrepreneurial aspects of reaching New Majority learners. Entrepreneurs thrive on finding underserved markets and designing products to meet these new or unmet needs.

No one wants to fold the tent overnight! Entrepreneurs know that if something isn't working, change it! But, to be successful, entrepreneurs know they have to be more than a fad, and they work tirelessly to build a stock of products to keep consumers, once engaged with their companies, both recommending them to others and coming back for more. A broad example of this is how fans devour such entertainment products as films, video games, streaming music on personal devices, live shows, all of which are entirely dependent on making an emotional connection with the consumer, and most significantly, making them feel special to keep buying the experience.

Think about it: In the academy, we develop degree programs we want to engage students in completing. We can deliver these to different audiences using differing formats. Further, we can create the sense of need for more by offering graduate degrees, continuing education, and certificate programs. And, like it or not, students really are consumers, especially New Majority students. They have to juggle personal economies on multiple levels; these appreciative inputs that influence student outputs may be grouped as time management, financial management, and effectively managing the systems and business practices of higher education.

This workshop's exercise invites you to do your own campus-specific planning to make New Majority learners "feel special" and to create what is sometimes called in the entertainment industry the "wow" experience—the one that touches your heart and makes you want to buy more of that feeling. We learn more about this in the chapter on student-centered learning design.

Osterwalder and Pigneur (2010) provide one of the clearest ways to launch a discussion of business models for beginners or seasoned entrepreneurs, which we want you to adapt to academic entrepreneurship. To find the key concepts and goals that inform a business proposition in a way that will lead to a business plan, they suggest you answer nine questions that refine your concept and create a SWOT, and they give you the necessary tools to evaluate the potential for success. If every academic program, with teams composed of faculty members, students, alums, employees, and staff, were to engage in program review, program development, or strategic planning using their model, with the New Majority learner as their customer, would this bring us closer to improving the business of education for these students? The only way to know is to try.

To gain a sense of how your institution is managing its inputs and outputs, Malm encourages clarity and articulating who you are and what makes you unique. As you realize, this is another way to approach Beth Rubin's argument from an applied perspective.

Activity

For this project, we will take the nine steps of business-model development and create a matrix to answer the questions. To keep us focused, we have started the project for you and adapted Osterwalder and Pigneur's guiding questions for this discussion:

- Who is my customer? The New Majority Learner (NML).
- What can we do, show, and tell NMLs that will make them value our institution over others?
- What do we need to deliver to NMLs?
- How can we build our reputation with NMLs?
- What money do NMLs generate for the institution?
- Where is this revenue coming from?
- What will assist the institution in successfully educating the NMLs?
- How will the institution market its academic programs to the NMLs?
- Who needs to help both NMLs and the institution create successful and sustained partnerships?
- How will the institution make money from changing or adding infrastructure to support NMLs?

These are respectively called customer segments, value propositions, value channels, customer relations, revenue streams, key resources, key activities, key partnerships, and the cost structure. Using a tool like http://www.liveplan.com, you and your teams can develop a working business plan that can be used to guide and integrate your steps in meeting the learning needs and professional aspirations of the New Majority learner.

Outcome

The outcome of creating an academic business plan is to articulate in easily understood language what you do, the layers of value that your institution offers, and what human and financial resources are needed to sustain the propositions on which your curriculum is structured for its intended beneficiaries.

Campus Book Group

Kelly, Andrew P., Jessica S. Howell, and Carolyn Sattin-Bajaj. *Matching Students to Opportunities. Expanding College Choice, Access, and Quality.* Cambridge, MA: Harvard Education Press, 2016.

Osterwalder, Alexander, and Yves Pigneur. *Business Model Generation: A Handbook for Visionaries, Game Changers, and Challengers.* Hoboken, NJ: Wiley, 2010.

Wacholtz, Larry. *Monetizing Entertainment. An Insider's Handbook for Careers in the Entertainment & Music Industry.* Edited by Beverly Schneller. London: Routledge, 2017.

CHAPTER 4: MORE THAN A FEELING

Marguerite Weber's chapter on learning design creates an opportunity for your campus to examine what it is doing in course and program review and in assessment of student learning outcomes. Should the learning outcomes change with the New Majority learner? What sort of instructional paradigms might be developed that would either disrupt current ways of thinking about student success or offer more depth for practices already in place? Let's start with a series of questions that will allow you to choose an entrance pathway into this conversation about learning design.

- How would you characterize ideas about the nature, scope, and experiences of learning on your campus?
- To what extent does your campus have an actual planned effort for achieving student learning outcomes?
- How would you express your campus's sense of "learning design"? For instance, do you have designated spaces and places for specific types of learning experiences? How do you staff such sites as your campus computer labs? What does your library look like from the learning-design perspective? Keep thinking about the "show" part of learning design. What else do you see?
- How does your campus use online learning as part of its learning theory and expectations for student success?
- What policies, if any, does your campus have for incorporating experiential learning, prior learning, badges, and other less traditional forms of learning into the student's degree plan? More importantly, does your campus have a plan for the future learning opportunities students may bring to your campus or have alternative credentials been planned for and accounted for in your campus leading models? Who are your campus leaders in these discussions?
- What are the costs to your campus for your current learning models? What are the costs of steps you would like to or need to take in the future to ensure high-quality instruction continues on your campus?
- To what degree have processes for new course and new program development been improved to accommodate pedagogies and learning outcomes reflective of academic transformations informed by knowledge of student learning needs?
- In what ways does it seem the data collected about student learning and student perceptions of learning could be used to inform learning design, course and program design, and academic-innovation conversations?

- How would you say your campus has responded to date to efforts at transformation, at any level?

Action Plan

The questions provided are worthy of deep and extended conversation. So, our first suggestion is pair a few of these into a research problem you want to pursue and then create campus stakeholder teams to inventory what your campus is doing, to find models of successful learning-design efforts that you believe your campus could implement or adapt, and then, create a modified business plan, as discussed in the prior workshop to see how you could profit and how you could benefit from adjustments to your current learning models.

Our second suggestion is to simultaneously form focus groups and one or more working groups of faculty, students, staff, and alums to work on the learning questions this chapter raises. Here are some ideas for the focus groups.

- How might you get and hold students' attention in the traditional classroom and in the online classroom? Matthew Crawford writes eloquently and provocatively about the "ethics of attention" and how the intellectual and emotional environments of competing demands on our attention render our abilities to set and achieve goals, make decisions, and function in the world, in general. (See the Campus Book Discussion for more on this.)
- How might you change students' ingrained beliefs (sometimes called *constructs*) about their learning abilities?
- How could you address faculty and student perceptions of peer learning support and supplemental instruction?
- How might you encourage students to take risks, the same risks your campus may be taking in academic transformation, and come with your faculty on the journey to create new learning designs for the New Majority learners?
- How can you add multiple approaches to the learning environment and manage resources at the same time? What networks exist or could be built to broaden access to other delivery and learning methods and tools?
- What grants might your campus pursue to support your efforts to enhance academic transformation? What incentives does your campus need to create or continue to support and encourage innovative course redesign and experimentation? How effective are the campus promotion, tenure, sabbatical, and annual-renewal reporting processes in rewarding innovation efforts, whether the results are deemed successful or less unsuccessful?

Outcomes

To be successful in redesigning anything, you have to have a budget and a plan. Simply, you will do better with something like home renovations if you have decided where to put your money, how much money you have and are willing to spend, and what you want the room or location to look like when you are done. Often, the goal of renovation is to make living more comfortable or to make it more aesthetically appealing. Why should we think differently about renovating the learning models on our campus?

Within our context, the aim of exploring learning design, learning theories, and related pedagogical approaches is twofold: (1) to understand what your campus is thinking and doing to support student leaning through supplemental instruction, online-augmented learning, and collaborations such as the emporium and the buffet models, and (2) to create a road map for meaningful academic transformation and most likely a rewritten "theory" of learning for your campus, informed by knowledge of what and how students both want to learn and say they learn best. Here, the work of Peter Brown, Ken Bain, and others like them, who link learning design to habits of mind, may be formative in your campus's thinking.

Campus Book Discussion

Bain, Ken. *What the Best College Students Do.* Cambridge, MA: Harvard University Press, 2012.

———. *What the Best College Teachers Do.* Cambridge, MA: Harvard University Press, 2004.

Brint, Steven, ed. *The Future of the City of Intellect: The Changing American University.* Redwood City, CA: Stanford University Press, 2002.

Brown, Peter. *Make It Stick: The Science of Successful Learning.* Cambridge, MA: Belknap Press, 2014.

Crawford, Matthew B. *The World Beyond Your Head: On Becoming an Individual in an Age of Distraction.* New York: Farrar, Straus, and Giroux, 2015.

CHAPTER 5: WILL YOU BE NUMBER ONE?

After the learning models are designed, implemented, and paid for in budget after budget, did we really win with the students? Did they get their needs met? Their degree? Their opportunity? Whose trophy is it?

To start our conversation, let's take a look at the roles we are currently playing on campus and our exercise is going to focus on statements of teaching philosophy and statements of learning philosophy as tools to help develop or extend access pedagogy. As Tomlinson-Keasey (2002) points out, when it comes to "weaving technology" into college learning, there are economic and sociological issues to be addressed, to which we add adaptive learning and persistence concerns, especially for adult and

New Majority learners (Brint 2002). Here are some big-picture discussion topics:

- The idea of access is evolving. Consider how LinkedIn, Facebook, Google, and other social media are assuming "instructional roles" by offering career-based courses and tutorials that are different from what is already available at Khan Academy, through Coursera, or the Penn State VLN, described in chapter 5. The full reach of artificial intelligence (AI) for educational purposes is not yet known, but analysis by Anand Rao for *Strategy+Business,* and articles in *Forbes* and *Fortune* give some idea of how commercial and consumer AI applications can be adapted for learning. What challenges and opportunities do these sources for learning present to your campus?
- What acknowledgment of changes in learning preferences do you find in your campus policies and in your teaching materials, such as a common syllabus, for example? If you have a teaching and learning center on campus, or focused professional development activities, are there distinct approaches in pedagogy and learning outcomes as they pertain to course-delivery methods? Do you have one set of directions and outcomes for online courses and one for face-to-face?
- What has been your campus experience with fully online learning? What are your persistence and graduation rates in any fully online or majority blended-learning programs? What is the DFW rate in online versus face-to-face classes? What questions does this examination of completion rates raise for you?

Design Activities

- A key to the success of the Cabrini adult-learning program is the blending of the high-touch peer mentoring with online and face-to-face instruction, which requires students to develop self-efficacy and learn from one another. Both of these outcomes are desirable to demonstrate to students that your institution wants them to succeed. Working in teams of four or five, use the following questions to create your own version of an adult-access program. How could you use the adaptive high-impact practices to create a similar program or programs on your campus? What will it cost to implement? What resources are on campus now and what would have to be added to create a similar program? How would you recruit for students? Who would find such a program most valuable? Would you be developing or creating new markets, or both? Your team may want to outline a business plan based on this exercise.

- Working in pairs using the think-pair-share model of discovery, before moving into larger teams, compose a statement of teaching philosophy for the VLN and for the Cabrini adult degree program. Take this opportunity to define and develop the roles of the faculty, the student, any learning support or supplemental instruction deemed integral, and the community or program alums. Create posters to showcase your statements and share with the larger group. How does this statement compare to others currently in use on your campus? Were there ways you need to think differently about your students and what you want them to experience on your campus as result of this activity? What is your next step with the results of this exercise?
- Your teams can probably think of a program that is unlikely to thrive digitally or maybe one that is underenrolling, that you want to save in light of staffing and budget pressures. What steps would you present to your campus to either convert an unlikely program into a VLN-style network of learning or redesign it to meet the needs of the New Majority and adult learners? Make a list and role-play the advocacy for your choice with "provost," "CFO," "dean," two faculty, and two or three "students." What did you learn?

Outcomes

Your campus may not be positioned to create a VLN, but you can no doubt imagine other ways you can network learning to maximize resources and human effort found in faculty, advisors, mentors, students, and staff. Similarly, your adaptive high-impact practices do not need to be solely for an adult student population. Teaching students through the "grand challenge" model, to develop their confidence as problem solvers, and to manage their time on task while meeting academic challenges are essential life skills, not just ones needed to pass a course. Adult and New Majority learners are potential campus leaders in these competencies and dispositions, having made their education the trophy they want to win. Let them be number one in your learning design, resource development, and institutional modeling, and you will naturally find a more robust engagement with the business of education on your campus.

Campus Book Discussion

Braxton, John, et al. *Rethinking College Student Retention*. San Francisco: Jossey-Bass, 2014.

Bowen, Jose. *Teaching Naked: How Moving Technology Out of Your Classroom Will Improve Student Learning*. Hoboken, NJ: Wiley, 2012.

Brint, Steven. *The Future of the City of Intellect: The Changing America University*. Redwood City, CA: Stanford University Press, 2002.

Friedman, Thomas L. *Thank You for Being Late: An Optimist's Guide to Thriving in the Age of Acceleration*. New York: Farrar, Straus, and Giroux, 2016.

Rao, Anand. "A Strategist's Guide to Artificial Intelligence," *Strategy+Business* (Summer 2017): 47–55.

Tomlinson-Keasey, Carol. "Becoming Digital: The Challenges of Weaving Technology throughout Higher Education." In *The Future of the City of Intellect: The Changing America University*, edited by Steven Brint, 133–58. Redwood City, CA: Stanford University Press, 2002.

CHAPTER 6: FILLING THE SEATS

Tim Jones's short and compelling piece in *Inside Higher Ed* (www. insidehighered.com), published June 22, 2017, acknowledges colleges and universities of all types are competing for the same pools of new and continuing students as a way of proposing collaboration as the means to healthy competition in the postsecondary market. Essentially, he sees collaboration leading to a kind of well-defined competition for access to the type of education a student seeks, attraction to particular types of programs chosen by the students, and awareness among institutions that if they can hook a student on going to college, it benefits the entire educational enterprise.

The entrepreneurial approaches to collaboration outlined in chapter 6 speak to what kinds of partnerships, pathways, and outcomes can be achieved when higher-education leadership, in particular, either capitalizes on the vision of its faculty, students, and staff or provides its own ways of extending the educational franchise to a diverse population of students.

Social psychologist Robert Caldini has a method we can apply here called "pre-suasion." The grounding element of pre-suasion is communicating in a way that combines influence with attention through which we create an interest in something "by arranging for recipients to be receptive to a message before they encounter it." He continues to explain by offering an experience or experiences that resonate with consumers (in his case), one creates the "likelihood" the consumer will be well disposed toward the idea, the product, or the opportunity. But what is really important about this, and especially to adult and New Majority learners, is that one's success in developing the likelihood is connected to the first experience the person has, the first encounter, and the first response. As with any good marketing strategy, the consumer/student needs to feel special, as though the event or activity is just for her, that the opportunity is something he or she will like or benefit from, that the opportunity is valid and supported by society or others, that the opportunity is established, and that there is something "scarce" or unique about the opportunity. If the persuader can match the identity of the persuaded with the opportunity, then the persuaded is considered "readied" for the opportunity. Pre-suasion creates the climate that leads the persuaded to change behaviors in such a way as to find meaning in the opportunity, to persist through it, and to adopt and adapt its outcomes for current and future uses.

Action Plan

For this workshop, we invite your campus teams to explore your "readiness" steps. What are you doing to make students feel special and how are you preparing them to navigate, accept, and thrive on your campus?

Outcomes

By expanding horizons to think about how you want your students to contribute to learning and living beyond the campus, you will want to review the pre- and per-suasive elements of who you say you are and what you can responsibly and ethically promise students as their experience of your campus.

Campus Book Discussion

Caldini, Robert. *Pre-Suasion: A Revolutionary Way to Influence and Persuade*. New York: Simon and Schuster, 2016.
Hora, Matthew T., with Ross J. Benbow and Amanda K. Oleson. *Beyond the Skills Gap: Preparing Students for Life and Work*. Cambridge, MA: Harvard Education Press, 2016.
Jones, Tim. "Beyond Competition: How Collaboration Helps Higher Ed," *Inside Higher Ed*, June 22, 2017, http://www.insidehighered.com.

CHAPTER 7: THE MEANING BEHIND STRATEGIC PLANNING

Call it planning, visioning, or discovering but in the end, the campus is continuously engaged in finding the next and, they hope, best courses of action, for the future. Michael Porter's work is perhaps the best known and most often used for strategic planning and is akin to Osterwalder and Pigneur in its ability to create a common currency for talking about strategy. In this chapter, authors Weber and Malm offer a way of thinking into a wide range of options for readiness to recruit, retain, and graduate multiple student groups and what the cost-benefit of casting a wider net brings to the campus.

Action Plan

Working in teams, create a storyboard or other large visual representation of your current strategic plan or goals, and together, map those goals onto what you have learned about learning design for the New Majority and the new educational landscapes. Be as thorough as possible, making note of the "grey" areas of uncertainty among your group as a measure of how effective your communication plan really is in helping all see common goals and means to a shared end.

Outcomes

By now, your campus should be comfortable struggling with how to think differently about financial aid, academic and residential policies, approaches to instructional design, continuous-improvement activities, and sustainability. This closing mapping exercise may be your road map to the future, allowing you to look at where you are going and if you carry the "where you have been" mind-set with you more than the "oh, the places we could go" perspective. Good luck!

Campus Book Discussion

Brighouse, Harry, and Michel McPherson. *The Aims of Higher Education: Problems of Morality and Justice.* Chicago: University of Chicago, 2015.

About the Editors

Eric Malm, associate professor of economics and business management and chair of the Business Department at Cabrini University in Radnor, Pennsylvania, provides the framework for understanding the New Majority as a specific group of learners. He has developed experiential hybrid classes, started his own marketing companies, and created policies and led training sessions on the role of technology in teaching and learning. Here, he outlines the demographic and traces the characteristics and needs of New Majority learners to open the way for exploring other issues addressed in this volume.

Marguerite Weber, is president of Higher Learning Design, a consulting firm that helps colleges and universities improve retention-centered practices across the student life cycle for diverse cohorts of students. Most recently she served as the vice president for student affairs at Baltimore City Community College. She has focused her professional career on both the learning needs of adult students and on designing appropriately flexible learning environments in and out of the classroom. She has served as the vice president for adult and professional programs at Cabrini University, has been an academic transformation fellow for the University System of Maryland, and has held teaching and administrative positions in Maryland, New York, and Pennsylvania. Her retention model, Fit/Fear/Focus, has informed first-year and bridge-program design as a way to engage students to persist as well as a vision for organizing the higher-education infrastructures to support diverse learners as they strive to achieve success. Here, she outlines academic and administrative redesign processes to improve effectiveness and sustainability.

About the Contributors

William A. Egan is an instructional designer for Penn State University's World Campus, where he specializes in designing and developing effective instruction for online and hybrid learning environments for a variety of graduate and undergraduate disciplines. Since 1998, the World Campus has offered unique value for adult learners, members of the military, and corporations seeking opportunities to increase workforce training and development. But the flexibility of online learning makes it an increasingly attractive option for students in the New Majority as well. In his chapter, he offers best practices for effective program design and decision making for faculty, IT professionals, instructional designers, and administrators that will enable them to create programs and courses that are appropriately structured and sequenced, clearly communicated, and accessible to a variety of users with differing learning needs.

Beth Rubin is dean of adult and online education (AEO) at Campbell University. After many years as a traditional academic, Dr. Rubin moved into academic administration in adult- and online-serving institutions, working in both for-profit and nonprofit arenas. She has conducted research on higher-educational systems and structures, the effects of learning management systems, the community of inquiry, and academic integrity. As dean of AEO, Dr. Rubin leads efforts to enhance learning and support for adult and remote students, overseeing multiple physical locations as well as online offerings. She collaborates with others to develop new undergraduate and graduate programs and oversees all aspects of instructional design, course development, instruction, student support, marketing, and back-end operations.

Beverly Schneller is professor of English at Belmont University in Nashville and former associate provost for academic affairs there. She is also a Teagle Assessment Scholar with the Center of Inquiry at Wabash College in Crawfordsville, Indiana. In addition to writing and publishing on literary topics and assessment of student learning, she is a consultant to colleges and universities on topics ranging from writing across the curriculum design and assessment to developing programs and curricula to enhance diversity.